AN ARTIST'S LETTERS
FROM JAPAN

JOHN LA FARGE

AN ARTIST'S LETTERS
FROM JAPAN

WATERSTONE · LONDON
HIPPOCRENE BOOKS · NEW YORK

Waterstone & Co. Limited
49 Hay's Mews
London WIX 7RT
Hippocrene Books, Inc.
171 Madison Ave.
New York, NY 10016

First published in Great Britain in 1897.

This edition first published 1986.

UK ISBN 0 947752 32 3
US ISBN 0 87052 302 3

Front Cover: Late nineteenth-century
Japanese textile design.
Reproduced by courtesy of the Board of
Trustees of the Victoria and Albert Museum,
London.

Cover design by Michael Head.

Printed and bound in Great Britain by
Richard Clay (The Chaucer Press) Ltd.,
Bungay, Suffolk.

To Henry Adams, Esq.

My Dear Adams: Without you I should not have seen the place, without you I should not have seen the things of which these notes are impressions. If anything worth repeating has been said by me in these letters, it has probably come from you, or has been suggested by being with you—perhaps even in the way of contradiction. And you may be amused by the lighter talk of the artist that merely describes appearances, or covers them with a tissue of dreams. And you alone will know how much has been withheld that might have been indiscreetly said.

If only we had found Nirvana—but he was right who warned us that we were late in this season of the world.

J. L. F.

AND YOU TOO, OKAKURA SAN: I wish to put your name before these notes, written at the time when I first met you, because the memories of your talks are connected with my liking of your country and of its story, and because for a time you were Japan to me. I hope, too, that some thoughts of yours will be detected in what I write, as a stream runs through grass — hidden, perhaps, but always there. We are separated by many things besides distance, but you know that the blossoms scattered by the waters of the torrent shall meet at its end.

CONTENTS

AN ARTIST'S LETTERS
FROM JAPAN

A RRIVED yesterday. On the cover of the letter which I
mailed from our steamer I had but time to write: "We
are coming in; it is like the picture books. Anything that I
can add will only be a filling in of detail."

We were in the great bay when I came up on deck in the
early morning. The sea was smooth like the brilliant blank
paper of the prints; a vast surface of water reflecting the light
of the sky as if it were thicker air. Far-off streaks of blue
light, like finest washes of the brush, determined distances.
Beyond, in a white haze, the square white sails spotted the
white horizon and floated above it.

The slackened beat of the engine made a great noise in the
quiet waters. Distant high hills of foggy green marked the
new land; nearer us, junks of the shapes you know, in violet
transparency of shadow, and five or six war-ships and
steamers, red and black, or white, looking barbarous and out
of place, but still as if they were part of us; and spread all
around us a fleet of small boats, manned by rowers standing
in robes flapping about them, or tucked in above their waists.
There were so many that the crowd looked blue and white —
the color of their dresses repeating the sky in prose. Still, the

larger part were mostly naked, and their legs and arms and backs made a great novelty to our eyes, accustomed to nothing but our ship, and the enormous space, empty of life, which had surrounded us for days. The muscles of the boatmen stood out sharply on their small frames. They had almost all—at least those who were young—fine wrists and delicate hands, and a handsome setting of the neck. The foot looked broad, with toes very square. They were excitedly waiting to help in the coaling and unloading, and soon we saw them begin to work, carrying great loads with much good-humored chattering. Around us played the smallest boats with rowers standing up and sculling. Then the market-boat came rushing to us, its standing rowers bending and rising, their thighs rounding and insteps sharpening, what small garments they had fluttering like scarfs, so that our fair missionaries turned their backs to the sight.

Two boys struggling at the great sculls in one of the small boats were called by us out of the crowd, and carried us off to look at the outgoing steamer, which takes our mail, and which added its own confusion and its attendant crowd of boats to all the animation on the water. Delicious and curious moment, this first sense of being free from the big prison of the ship; of the pleasure of directing one's own course; of not understanding a word of what one hears, and yet of getting at a meaning through every sense; of being close to the top of the waves on which we dance, instead of looking down upon them from the tall ship's sides; of seeing the small limbs of the boys burning yellow in the sun, and noticing how they recall the dolls of their own country in the expression of their eyes; how every little detail of the boat is different, and yet so curiously the same; and return to the first sensation of feeling while lying flat on the bottom of the boat, at the level of our faces the tossing sky-blue water dotted with innumerable orange copies of the sun. Then subtle influences of odor, the

2

sense of something very foreign, of the presence of another race, came up with the smell of the boat.

We climbed up the side of the big steamer and found the Doctor there, who told us that he had been expecting us for a whole month; so that he soon took possession of us, and we found ourselves in the hotel launch, and at the wharf, and passing the custom house and its officers, who let everything go through quickly except my suspicious water-color blocks. Outside of the gate, in the street, we found the long-expected *jinrikisha*, an arrangement that you know probably as well as I do—a two-wheeled perambulator or gig, very small, with a hood that is usually lowered, and with a man in the shafts. Our fellows were in blue-black clothes, a big inscription on their backs; and they wore apron-like vests, close-fitting trousers, and broad straw hats poised on their heads. But you know all about these; and I have only to add that we were trundled off to our hotel, along the pretty quay which edges that part of the town, past European houses, unlike ours, and having a certain character which will probably appear very commonplace later, because it is not beautiful, but which is novel yet to us. Our hotel is also on the quay, just at a corner where a canal breaks in, and where we can see big walls and trees on the other side. Our rooms open on the water—that same blue water spangled with sunshine and fading into sky. There are men-of-war and steamers far out; picturesque junks sailing past rapidly, flattened out into mere edges of shadow and light against the sea and the sky, their great hollow sterns with the rudder far inboard, and sails which are open at the seams. Not far from us was a little sharp-pointed boat with a man fishing, his big round hat as important as any part of the boat. It was already late in the day. European children were out with their Japanese nurses; from time to time a phaeton or a curricle passed with European occupants, and even in this tremendous heat ladies rode out

3

on horseback. But the human beings are not the novelty, not even the Japanese; what is absorbingly new is the light, its whiteness, its silvery milkiness. We have come into it as though an open door after fourteen gray days of the Pacific which ended only at sunrise this very morning. And we looked again at all the light outside, from the dining-room, where we lunched, where the waiters slipped about in black clothes like those of the runners, and where we were joined at table by a foreign gentleman with high cheek-bones, yellow face, and slanting eyes, and dressed in the latest European fashion with high collar, four-in-hand scarf, and pointed shoes. He was very courteous, and managed what little English he used as skilfully as he dresses. And he gave me a touch of the far East in the story of his being here; for he is under a cloud, an amiable exile whose return to his native land might involve his being boiled in oil, or other ingenious form of death. For well as he figured at luncheon with us, I hear that he has been obliged to leave because of his having poisoned too many of his guests one day at table—former enemies of his,—and because of his having despatched with the sword those whose digestion had resisted his efforts at conciliation. However this may be, his extradition is demanded; to which he objects, invoking Western ideas of civilization, and protesting that his excesses have been merely political. Then, late in the afternoon, we sauntered out into the Japanese quarter—walking, so that we might mingle with the gray, black, and blue crowd, and respectfully followed by our jinrikisha men, who slowly dragged our carriages behind them, like grooms following their masters. We stopped at little curio shops and bargained over miserable odds and ends, calling up, I feel sure, the unexpressed contempt of the Doctor, the great collector of precious lacquers; but it is so amusing to see things as they are, and not as they should be. We went into a show which had an enormous draped sign

4

outside, and where, in uncertain darkness, an old, miserable, distorted dwarf played the part of a spider in a web, to the accompaniment of fiendish music and the declamation of the showman. Then we lingered outside of a booth in which a wrestling match was going on, but did not enter, and we saw the big wrestlers go in or come out, their shoulders far above the heads of a smaller race of men, and we turned at every moment to look at the children, many of whom are so pretty, and who seem to have an easy time of it. Men carry them in their arms as women do with us, and many a little elder sister walks about with the infant of the family slung behind her maternal shoulders. And then there are curious combinations of Western and Eastern dress — rarely successful. Our hats and shoes and umbrellas — all made here, are used, and our ugly shirts stiffen out the folds of the soft Japanese robes; but the multitude wear their usual dress and make no abuse of hats.

Wearied by the novelty, every detail of which, however, was known to us before, we walked back in the white, milky sunset, which was like a brilliant twilight.

JULY 5.

We made our first visit to town yesterday; that is to say, we went to Tokio, which is about twenty miles off. Of course we took our *jinrikishas* at the door of the hotel, and passing through the wide Yokohama streets, saw the semi-European houses, some with high garden walls in which are small doors; there are sidewalks, too, and European shops, and Colonial buildings, post-office, and telegraph office; and the Japanese *kura*, or storehouses — heavy tile-roofed buildings with black and white earthen surfaces, the black polished to a glaze, as was done with Greek and Etruscan vases. They have deep windows or doors, recessed like our safes, with a great air of solidity, which contrasts with that temporary wooden structure, the usual Japanese house. I came near saying that the little railway station is like ours; but it is better than most of ours, with neat arrangements. We entered the little cars; I noticed, in the third class, Japanese curled up on the seats. The grade is as level as a table, the landscape is lovely, and we saw the shapes we know so well in the prints—the curious shapes of the Japanese pines; little temples on the hillside; and rice-fields with their network of causeways, occasionally a horse or a peasant threading them. The land is cultivated like a garden, the lotus leaves fill the ditches, and one or two pink flowers are just out. From time to time we saw stretches of blue sea. And once, for an instant, as I looked up into the hazy, clouded sky, far beyond the hills, that were lost in the mist into which the rice-field stretched, I saw a pale, clear blue opening in which was an outline more distinct, something very pure, the edge of a mountain, looking as if it belonged to another world than the dewy moist one in which we are—the cone of Fusi-yama.

On passing through the station, very much like the other with its various arrangements for comfort and order,—first, second, and third-class rooms, and so forth,—we met a crowd of *jinrikishas* with their runners, or, as my friends tell me to call them, *kuruma* and *kurumaya*, every man clamoring for patronage in the usual way of the hackman.

We selected as a leader Chojiro, who speaks English—a little; is a traveled man, having gone as far as Constantinople; wears the old-fashioned queue, flattened forward over the top of his shaven head; and whose naked feet were to run through the day over newly-macadamized roads, for which a horse would need to be well shod. A little way from us, on the square, stood the car of the tramway, which runs as far as Asakusa, to the great popular temples of protecting divinities, Kuwanon and Jizo,—and Benten, from whose shrine flowed one day copper coins as if from a fountain,—where Buddhist

6

sermons are preached daily; which are full of innumerable images, pictures, and ex-votos; and where prayer-wheels, duly turned, helped the worshiper to be free from annoying sins, or to obtain his desires.

How shall I describe our ride through the enormous city? We were going far across it to call on Professor F——, the great authority on Japanese art, and to be delighted and instructed by him through some fragments of his collection.

In the first street where the tramway runs there are semi-European façades to houses, and in their pilasters the Ionic capital has at length made the circle of the world. Then we took more Oriental and narrower streets, through the quarter of the *gei-sha*, the dancers and singers who go out perpetually to put a finishing touch on entertainments. At such early hours they are of course unseen. Where houses seemed more closed than usual servants were attending to household duties, and we heard the occasional strum of a guitar. Then great streets again, with innumerable low houses, the usual shops, like open sheds, with swinging signs carved, painted, and gilded, or with draperies of black cloth marked with white characters. Merchants sat on their mats among the crowded goods, girls at corners drew water from the wells; in a narrower street the black streak of a file of bulls peacefully dragging merchandise; where the crowd was thickest a black-lacquered palanquin, all closed, in which was shut some obstinate adherent to ancient fashions. Then bridges and canals, and great empty spaces, long white walls with black copings, and buildings that continued the walls, with gratings like those of barracks. These were the *yashikis*—inclosed residences of princes who were formerly obliged to spend part of the year at the seat of government with small armies of retainers. Then the walls of the castle, great sloping ramparts of irregular blocks of masonry, about which stand strangely twisted pine-trees, while the great moats of clouded water are almost filled with the big leaves of the lotus. Now and then great gates of gray wood and enormous doors. On some of the wide avenues we met cavalry officers in European costume, correct in style, most of the younger with straggling mustaches, long and thin, whence their nickname of "horn-pouts", naturally connected with that of the "cats", devourers of fish, as the *gei-sha* are called. Near official buildings we saw a great deal of black frock-coats, and trousers, and spectacles. Everything was seen at a full run, our runners dragging us at horse's pace. Still it was long before we reached our destination. Streets succeeded streets, empty or full, in desolate Oriental wearisomeness. At length we stopped at a little gate in a plank fence, and entered a vast high space, formerly a prince's park, at one end of which we saw trees and hills, and we came to the Professor's house, a little European structure. My mind is yet too confused with many impressions to tell you of what we saw that afternoon and evening, and what was said; all the more that the few beautiful paintings we looked at out of the great collection lifted me away from to-day into an indefinite great past. I dislike to use analogies, but before these ancient religious paintings of Buddhist divinities, symbolical of the elements or of protective powers, whose worn surfaces contained marvels of passionate delicacy and care framed in noble lines, I could not help the recall of what I had once felt at the first sight of old Italian art.

We passed from this sense of exalted peace to plunge again into the crowded streets at night. It was late; we had many miles to go to catch the last train; two additional runners had been engaged for each *kuruma*—one to push, one to be harnessed in front.

Then began a furious ride. Mine was the last carriage. We were whirled along with warning cries of "Hai-hai!" now into the dark, then into some opening lighted by star-light, in which I could see the flitting shapes of the other runners and of my companions. I remember the creaking of their carriages, the jerking of them with each pull of the men; then our crossing suddenly other parties lighted by lanterns like ourselves, the lights flaring upon yellow faces and dark dresses and black hair; then our turning some narrow corner and plunging at full speed into lighted streets crowded with people, through whom we seemed to cut our way. Much shouting of our men, and dodging of wayfarers with lanterns and of bystanders who merely turn enough to let us glide by. Then one of my runners at full gallop struck a post and was left behind; another was gathered in somehow without a stop, and we tore through the city, still more crowded as we came nearer to our end—the railway station. We were in time, and we slept in the now familiar train. We reached the deserted station and were jogged peacefully to our hotel; our men, in Japanese fashion, sleepily turning out of the way of the ownerless dogs that lay in the middle of the streets. And when I awoke in the morning I found that the day's impressions had faded in sleep to what I tell you.

JULY 6.

I have been asking myself whether it would be possible to have sensations as novel, to feel as perfectly fresh, things I knew almost all about beforehand, had we come in any other way, or arrived from any other quarter. As it is, all this Japan is sudden. We have last been living at home, are shut up in a ship, as if boxed in with our own civilization, and then suddenly, with no transition, we are landed in another. And under what splendor of light, in what contrasting atmosphere! It is as if the sky, in its variations, were the great subject of the drama we are looking at, or at least its great chorus. The beauty of the light and of the air is what I should like to describe, but it is almost like trying to account

9

for one's own mood — like describing the key in which one plays. And yet I have not begun to paint, and I dread the moment of beginning to work again. Rather have I felt like yielding entirely to the spirit in which I came, the intention of a rest, of a bath for the brain in some water absolutely alien. A——and I had undertaken that we should bring no books, read no books, but come as innocently as we could; the only compromise my keeping a scientific Japanese grammar, which, being ancient and unpractical, might be allowed, for it would leave me as unready as on the day I left.

The Doctor took us on Sunday afternoon to his club — whose name I think means the perfume of the maple — to see and to listen to some Japanese plays which are given in the club theater built for the purpose. We went there in the afternoon, passing by the Shiba temples, and our *kurumas* were drawn up at one end of the buildings. There everything was Japanese, though I hear stories of the other club and its ultra-European ways — brandies-and-sodas, single eye-glasses, etc. However that may be, on this side we were in Japan without mistake. We sat on the steps and had our shoes taken off, according to the Japanese fashion, so as not to injure mats, and we could hear during the operation long wailings, high notes, and the piercing sound of flutes and stringed instruments; the curiously sad rhythm mingled with a background of high, distinct declamation. We walked in with careful attention to make no noise, forgetting that in our stocking-feet we could have made none had we wished, and we found the Doctor's place reserved for him and us, and marked with his name, written large. Other low boxes, with sides no higher than our elbows as we sat on the mats, divided the sloping floor down to the stage. The stage was a pretty little building projecting into the great hall from its long side. It had its own roof, and connected with a long gallery or bridge, along which the actors moved, as they came on or disappeared, in a manner new to us, but which gave a certain natural sequence and made a beginning and an end, — a dramatic introduction and conclusion, — and added greatly to the picture when the magnificent dresses of stiff brocade dragged slowly along to the cadence of the music. The boxes were mostly occupied, and by a distinguished-looking audience; the Nǫ, as this operatic acting is called, being a refined, classical drama, and looked upon differently from the more or less disreputable theater. Hence the large proportion of ladies, to whom the theater is forbidden. Hence, also, owing to its antiquity and the character of its style, a difficulty of comprehension for the general public that explained the repeated rustle of the books of the opera which most of the women held, whose leaves turned over at the same moment, just as ours used to do at home when we were favored by French tragedy.

A quiet, sleepy appreciation hovered over the scene; even the devotees near us, many of them older people and belonging to the old régime, showing their approval or disapproval with restrained criticism. I could see without turning my head the expression of the face of my neighbor, a former *daimio*, a man of position; his face a Japanese translation of the universal well-known aristocratic type — immovable, fatigued, with the drooping under lip. Behind him sat former retainers, I suppose — deferential, insinuating remarks and judgments, to which he assented with inimitable brevity. Still, I thought that I could distinguish, when he showed that the youthful amateurs — for most of the actors were non-professional — did not come up to a proper standard, that his memory went back to a long experience of good acting. And so catching are the impressions of a crowd that I myself after a time believed that I recognized, more or less distinctly, the tyro and the master, even though I only vaguely understood what it was all about. For I need not tell you that the libretto would have been still more difficult for me than the pantomime before me; and very often it was but pantomime, the actor making gestures to the accompaniment of music, or of the declaration of the choragus, who told the poetic story. Occasionally these movements amounted to a dance, that is to say, to rhythmic movements—hence called the *Nō* dance—to which emphasis was given by rising and falling on either foot, and bringing down the sole with a sudden blow.

There were many short plays, mostly based on legendary subjects, distinguished by gorgeous dresses, and occasionally some comic scenes of domestic life. The monotony of impression was too novel to me to become wearisome, and I sat for several hours through this succession of separate stories, patient, except for the new difficulty of sitting cross-legged on the mats. Moreover, we had tobacco to cheer us. On our arrival the noiseless servants had brought to us the inevitable little tray containing the fire-box with hot charcoal and the little cylinder for ashes, and tea and little sugary balls; and then, besides, notwithstanding the high-toned repose of the audience, there was enough to watch. There were the envoys from Loo Choo, seated far off in the dim light of the room, dressed in ancient costumes, their hair skewered up on the top of the head with a double pin—grave and dignified personages; and a European prince, a Napoleonic pretender, seated alongside, with his suite, and ourselves, the only foreigners. The types of the older people were full of interest, as one felt them formed under other ideas than those of to-day. And though there were no beauties, there were much refinement and sweetness in the faces of the women, set off by the simplicity of their dresses, of blacks, and browns, and grays, and dull violets, in exquisite fabrics, for we were in an atmosphere of good breeding. And I watched one of the young ladies in front of me, the elder of two sisters, as she attended to every little want of her father, and even to his inconveniences. And now it was time to leave, though the performance was still going on, for we wished to return in the early evening. Our shoes were put on again at the steps, our umbrellas handed to us—for sun and rain we must always have one—and we passed the Shiba temples and took the train back for Yokohama.

JULY 12.

We are doing nothing in particular, hesitating very much as to what our course shall be. One thing is certain—the breaking out of the cholera will affect all our plans. Even the consequent closing of the theaters shows us how many things will be cut off from us. We spend much time in such idleness as bric-à-brac, letting ourselves go, and taking things as they come.

The Doctor's kindness is with us all the time. One feels the citizen of the world that he is when he touches little details of manners here, now as familiar to him as those of Europe.

I enjoy, myself, this drifting, though A—— is not so well pleased, and I try to feel as if the heat and the novelty of impressions justified me in idleness. Once only I was tempted to duty, however, when we went to the temples of Shiba and Uyèno, where are the tombs of the shoguns, rulers of Japan of the Tokugawa line. They are all there but the two greatest, Iyéyasŭ and Iyémitsŭ, who lie at Nikko, the sacred place, a hundred miles away. Here in Tokio are the tombs of the others, and the temples about them splendid with lacquer and carving and gold and bronze, and set among trees and gardens on these hills of the Shiba and Uyèno.

My dreams of making an analysis and memoranda of these architectural treasures of Japan were started, as many

13

resolutions of work are, by the talk of my companion, his analysis of the theme of their architecture, and my feeling a sort of desire to rival him on a ground for fair competition. But I do not think that I could grasp a subject in such a clear and dispassionate and masterly way, with such natural reference to the past and its implied comparisons, for A——'s historic sense amounts to poetry, and his deductions and remarks always set my mind sailing into new channels.

But I must put this off—certainly for to-day—while we discuss whether we shall make our visit to ancient Kamakura and the great bronze statue and the island of Énoshima, or whether to put it off until our return from Nikko, and our seeing the other shrines of the shoguns there. The Doctor, who has just left Nikko, tells us of its beauty in the early summer, a few weeks ago, and I feel all the hotter as he talks of the cold mountian streams which run by his house and of banks of azaleas covering the high rocks. And then the Japanese proverb says, "Who has not seen Nikko cannot say beautiful."

FROM TOKIO TO NIKKO

July 20, 1886.

THE cholera was upon us, and we decided to go to Nikko and spend a month there, near the F——s'. The Doctor, who was anxious to get back to its coolness and its other charms, was to pilot us and instruct us by the way, and much of the miscellaneous information that I shall give you has come more or less from him. Late in the morning we rode to Tokio, and lunched in Uyèno Park, looking down on the great pond and the little temple which stands in it, and which you know, having seen them on the fans and colored prints. They were veiled in the haze of the sunlight, as if in a spring or winter mist, and through this fog of light shone the multitudinous little sparkles of the ribs and swellings of the lotus-pads lapping one over another, and reaching to far streaks of clearer water. A denser lightness here and there marked the places of the flowers, and a faint odor came up in lazy whiffs. The roof of the temple seemed to be supported by the moisture below. Above there was no cloud. All things lay alike in the blaze, enveloped in a white glimmer of heat and wet, and between the branches of the trees around us the sky was veiled in blue. The locusts hissed with a crackling sound like that of heated wood. The ugly bronze Buddha at the corner of the tea-house shone as if melting in the sun. Then came the moment of leaving for the station, where, owing to delays of trains, we waited still longer in the heat. In the cleanly waiting-room we looked at the illustrations in the Japanese newspapers, and at the last report of the weather

15

bureau, printed in English and fastened to the wall; or we read a little in that morning's edition of the excellent Yokohama English paper; all these comforts of civilization being supplied by the Road. At length the noise of hundreds of wooden clogs, worn by men, women, and children, clattered upon the stones outside and announced an end to waiting. The tightly-closed train had been baking in the sun all day, and we leaned out of the doors on the sides and gasped for breath.

Our train skirted the great hill of Uyèno, and its dark shadow, which did not quite reach us. Monuments and gravestones, gray or mossy, blurred here and there the green wall of trees. The Doctor told us of the cooler spring-time, when the cherry-trees of Uyèno cover the ground with a snow of blossoms, and the whole world turns out to enjoy them, as we do the first snows of winter.

But this is a lame comparison. The Japanese sensitiveness to the beauties of the outside world is something much more delicate and complex and contemplative, and at the same time more natural, than ours has ever been. Outside of Arcadia, I know of no other land whose people hang verses on the trees in honor of their beauty; where families travel far before the dawn to see the first light touch the new buds. Where else do the newspapers announce the spring openings of the blossoms? Where else would be possible the charming absurdity of the story that W—— was telling me of having seen in cherry-blossom time some old gentleman, with capacious sakè gourd in hand and big roll of paper in his girdle, seat himself below the blossom-showers, and look, and drink, and write verses, all by himself, with no gallery to help him? If there is convention in a tradition half obligatory; and if we, Western lovers of the tree, do not quite like the Japanese refinement of growing the cherry merely for its flowers, yet how deliciously upside-down from us, and how charming is the love of nature at the foundation of the custom!

From the rustling of leaves and reëchoing of trees we passed into the open country, and into free air and heat. In the blur of hot air, trembling beneath the sun, lay plantations and rice-fields; the latter, vast sheets of water dotted with innumerable spikes of green. Little paths raised above them made a network of irregular geometry. Occasionally a crane spread a shining wing and sank again. In the outside ditches stood up the pink heads of the lotus above the crowded pads. At long intervals small groups of peasants, men and women, dressed in blue and white, knee-deep in the water, bent their backs at the task of weeding. The skirts of their dresses were caught up in their girdles, and their arms were freed from their looped-back sleeves.

The Doctor spoke to us of the supposed unhealthiness of rice-planting, which makes life in the rice-fields short, in a country where life is not long.

We are told that the manuring of the rice-fields taints all the waters for great distances, and we are warned not to drink, without inquiring, even from the clearest streams. Not even high up in the mountains shall we be safe; for there may be flat spaces and table-lands of culture which drain into the picturesque wildness below. We learn that with all these hardships the rice-growers themselves cannot always afford this staple food of the country, for cheaper than rice are millet, and buckwheat, and the plants and fungi that grow without culture.

Contrasting with the tillage we were passing, islands of close foliage stood up in the dry plain, or were reflected, with the clouds above, in the mirror of the wet rice-fields. Occasionally a shrine was visible within, and the obligatory Torii stood at the edge of the grove, or within its first limits.

Looking through a Torii one is sure to be in the direction of something sacred, whether it be temple or shrine or holy mountain. Neither closeness nor distance interferes with this ideal intention, and the sacred Fusi-yama is often seen a hundred miles away in the sky, framed by these lines, built for the purpose. This assemblage of four lines of stone or wood or bronze is to me one of the creations of art, like the obelisk or the pyramid. Most impressive, most original of symbolic entrances, whether derived from sacred India or from the ancestral innocence of Polynesia, there is something of the beginning of man, something invented while he lived with the birds, in this elementary porch, whose upper line, repeating the slope of hill and wave, first embodied the curve that curls all upper edges in the buildings of the farther East.

And if, indeed, the Torii[1] be nothing but the first bird-perch, then I can imagine the father of all peacocks spreading his gigantic fan across its bars; or I may prefer to suppose it the rest for the disk of the sun-god, whose lower curve is repeated by the Torii's upper beam.

Sometimes there were traces of inclosure about these woods; sometimes they had no edgings but their own beautifully-modeled contours. Long ages, respectful care, sometimes fortunate neglect, have made of these reserved spaces types of an ideal wildness, for these are sacred groves, and they are protected by the divine contained within them.

This preservation of a recall of primeval nature, this exemption of the soil from labor, within anxious and careful tillage, is a note of Japan constantly recurring, and a source of perpetual charm.

Notwithstanding the men and women working in the fields, there was a certain desolateness in the landscape, and A—— made out its reason more easily than I, and recalled that for miles and miles we had traveled without seeing any of the four-footed beasts which the Western mind always associates with pastoral life and labor.

[1] The usual etymology of Torii is bird-perch; from *Tori*, a bird.

As the evening came on we crossed a large river and looked down from the height of the new bridges upon the discarded ferry-boats, and upon the shape of a more fantastic one that was never meant to sail—a pine-tree, shaped and trimmed, which spread its green mast and sails in a garden by the water. Far away were lines of mountains and the peaks of extinct volcanoes.

At every station now the country people gathered to stare at the novelty of the train; we saw the lighting up of the farm-houses as we passed; in the dooryards, behind high hedges reminding me of Normandy, bonfires were being made to keep off mosquitoes: then temples and shrines with lights before them, and at eight o'clock on a festal night we came into Utsunomiya.

The streets were full of people carrying lanterns; children ran about together, with little toy shrines, and the whole town was drowned in noise. We got into a *basha*, a sort of omnibus, attached to two wild horses, and were hurled through the crowded streets, much as if carrying the mails, with apparent disregard of the lives and limbs of the inhabitants.

The hotel, where we were expected and where the Doctor had represented us as distinguished visitors, opened its whole front, in a Japanese way, to receive us, for there was no outside wall to the lower floor. We were driven quite into the house, and beheld an entire household drawn up in line on the platform, which occupied a full half of this lower space. The Doctor did all that was right, while we remained in amused embarrassment before our prostrated host and the kneeling attendants. As we sat helpless on the steps of the platform our shoes were taken off, and in stockinged feet we were ushered through the crowd and the lower part of the house, through the preparations for passing travelers, the smell and heat of washing and cookery, and an inexpressibly

19

outrageous odor, even for this land of frightful smells, evidently of the same nature as that of the rice-fields.

Notwithstanding this horror, we found, on clambering up the steep little staircase of dark, slippery wood, better fitted to stockings than to boots, a most charming, cleanly apartment ready for us: ready, I say, but its three big rooms, which took all one side of the court, contained nothing but a drawing hanging in each room and a vase filled with flowers; in justice, I ought to add a European table of the simplest make, and three European chairs. Under them was spread a piece of that red cloth which seems to have a fascination for the Japanese—perhaps as being European.

Everything was of the cleanest—wall, floor, stairs, tables; everything was dusted, wiped, rubbed, polished.

It was too hot and we were too tired to go out and see the town, noisy with the excitement of a festival. The Doctor directed the preparation of a meal on a Japanese basis of rice, mingled and enlivened with the contents of various cans; and meanwhile I went down another little staircase of cleanly white wood, at the farther end of our apartment, to our little private bath-room below.

This was about six feet square, and its furniture consisted of a deep lacquer tray to lay clothes in. The bath-tub was sunk in the floor, but so that its edges rose high above the level of the room. I had declined the "honorable hot water," which is the Japanese necessity, and obtained cold, against protest. I had yet to learn the luxury and real advantage of the Japanese hot bath. I closed my door, but my window was open, and through its wooden bars I could see our opposite neighbors across the garden of the courtyard—a whole family, father, mother, children, and young daughter—file down to the big bath-room at the corner, whose windows were open to mine. I heard them romp and splash, and saw heads and naked arms shining through the steam. Meditating upon the differences which make propriety in various places, I joined my friends at dinner and listened to what the Doctor had to say upon the Japanese indifference to nudity; how Japanese morals are not affected by the simplicity of their costumes, and that, of course, to the artist it seems a great pity that the new ideas should be changing these habits in a race so naturally law-abiding; for even the government is interfering, and enforcing dress within city limits. Then came the question whether this be a reminiscence of Polynesian ancestry and simplicity, or born of climate and cleanliness. And, indeed, all Japan spends most of its time washing, so that the very runners bathe more times a day than our fine ladies. Meanwhile the servant-girls were spreading for us the blue-green mosquito nettings, put together with bands of orange silk. They were slung by cords from the corners of the beams, which serve for a cornice, and they made a good-sized square tent in the middle of the room. Inside, our beds were made up on the floor, of well-wadded coverlets folded one upon another. One of these I took for a pillow. I have not yet dared to try the block of wood, hollowed out for the nape of the neck, which serves for a pillow in Japan, notwith-standing that it has a pad to relieve its severity—a pad of paper fastened on, and which you remove sheet by sheet as you want a clean pillow-slip. I can understand, however, how precious it must be in a country where the women keep, day and night, undisturbed, those coiffures of marvellous black hair, glistening with camellia oil, the name of which I like better than its perfume. From inside my netting I could see, as I was lying,—for the screens, which made our windows, remained wide open,—through the topmost branches of the trees of the garden, the Japanese family opposite, now ending their evening meal.

Laughter and chatter, clattering of cups, rap of pipes against boxes, a young man came in and bent over one of the women seated upon the floor; the girl repeated some prayer, with clapping hands outstretched; the lights were put out, all but the square "ando," or floor night-lantern, and they drew their screens. I fell asleep, to be waked with a start by the watchman, who, every hour, paced through the garden, striking a wooden clapper, and impertinently assured us of the hour.

This weary noise marked the intervals of a night of illness, made worse by nightmares of the cholera, from which we were flying. The earliest dawn was made hideous by the unbarring and rolling of the heavy *amados*,[1] the drawing back of the inside screens (*shojis*), and the clattering of clogs over pavement, through other parts of the house. Our Japanese family across the way I could hear at their ablutions, and, later, tumultuously departing for early trains; and at last I slept in broad daylight.

Late in the morning we entered our friend the *basha*. In the daylight I noticed that the horses wore something like a Dutch collar, and were harnessed with ropes. Two men, one the driver, the other the running groom, sat on the low front seat. Our trunks and bags and Japanese baskets encumbered the omnibus seats, on which we stretched our sick and wearied bodies, for the Doctor himself was ill, and smiled mechanically when I tortured him with questions. We left town at a full gallop, and at risk of life for every one in the streets; one of our drivers meanwhile blowing wildly through a horn, to the inspiriting of the horses and the frightening of the Japanese small-boy. Soon one of our men plunged off his seat and began running by the horses in the old Japanese way—hereditary with him, for they follow the calling from

[1] Rain-doors, outer wooden screens, which close the house at night, and roll in a groove.

generation to generation. Running without pause and without sweating, he threw his body back as if restraining his pace to that of the horses. At the limits of the town, in full run, he stripped his upper garments and showed himself tattooed at every visible point. Above the double strip of his breech-clout, a waterfall, a dragon, and a noble hero made a fine network of blue and pink on the moving muscles.

Now the road became heavy, wet, and full of deep ruts, and out miserable ponies came to a standstill—and balked. The Japanese mildness of our driver disappeared. He took to beating their poor backs with a heavy bamboo cane, while we remonstrated feebly, regretting that we had not sufficient strength to beat him too. Then he explained, deferentially, that confusion seized him at being unable to keep his promise of delivering us to Imaichi for the appointed hour, and I felt as if we had been put in the wrong. Imagine the difference had he been—any one but a Japanese. We turned aside from the main way into a little dry side-path, which led us into the hills and moors. As we got among them we left the annoying odors of the rice-fields and smelled for the first time the fragrance of wild roses, looking like ours, but a little paler. This was the first thing which reminded me of home—the roses that the Japanese do not seem to care for, do not seem to understand. With them the rose has no records, no asso-ciations, as with us; for, once on this farther side of the garden of Iran, the peony and the chrysanthemum, the lotus and the iris, the peach, the cherry, and the plum, make up the flower-poetry of the extreme East.

Then, leaving the dry and sunny uplands, we entered a famous avenue, shaded for twenty miles by gigantic cryp-tomeria trees 60 to 120 feet high. They were planted as an act of homage, some two centuries ago, by some mighty noble, when it was decided to place at Nikko the tomb of the great

23

shogun Iyéyasǔ. They rise on each side of the sunken road, from banks and mounds, over which steps lead, from time to time, to plantations and rice-fields beyond, and to shrines peeping out among the trees. In side-roads above, on either hand, passed occasionally peasants and pack-horses laden with forage, or the bright shine of a peasant woman's red skirt. Where an occasional habitation, or two or three, are niched in some opening, the tall columns of the great trees are interrupted by spaces filled with crossed branches of the wilder pine; and behind these, outside, sometimes the light-green feathery mass of a bamboo grove. Against the bank stood low, thatched buildings; near them the great trees were often down, or sometimes dying; an occasional haystack, sliced off below by use, was fastened, in thick projection, around some smaller tree. Once, at a turn of the road, near a building with wide roof, pushed against the corner bank out of a basin fringed with iris, sprang into the air a little jet of water. Near by, a solitary ditcher had placed in a bamboo fence some bright red blossom, with its stem and leaves, apparently to cheer him at his work.

The heavy road was being ditched on each side to carry off the soaking waters, and our weary, miserable horses broke down again. A—— and I rested by going in advance, and I experienced the new sensation of walking among the bamboo stems, like an insect among the knotted stalks of a gigantic grass. The still heat of the sun burned in great smoky streaks across our way, spotted by the flight of many yellow butter-flies. There was no sound of birds in the high spaces above; the few peasants that we met slipped past on their straw sandals, their noiseless horses also shod with straw; occasion-ally a shiver of the great spruces overhead, and far behind us the cries of our grooms to their horses.

It was two o'clock when we galloped bravely, as if with fresh horses, into the single long street which is Imaichi

24

village. We were now on high ground, some two thousand feet above out point of departure, and could feel, but not see clearly, in the blaze of sunlight, great mountains lost in great wet clouds.

We stopped at the village inn; drivers and runners were sitting on the stone bench in front, drinking tea, when we drove up. We sat down on the straw-matted porch inside, the whole front of the building open, and drank miserable, herby tea, and tasted the usual sweet balls of sugary stuff.

Alongside the tea-house, in one of the recesses between the buildings, we could see the runners of *kurumas* being washed off and rubbed down, just as if they were horses in a livery stable. As they stood naked, their companions poured pails of water over them, its brown spread covering the stone slabs. Some of them, in the porch, lay on their backs, others prone, others on the side, all near a kettle, which hung over a charcoal fire, in which, perhaps, they were heating sakè. One on his back, his neck on the wooden pillow, was smoking. The village itself lay in hot, clean repose,—not dusty,—the rows of buildings on each side of the street irregular, but all of the same appearance. Most of the fronts were open, the goods all displayed outside of the walls, or on the floors, innumerable pieces of paper hanging about everywhere. A few men sat about on the porches, their naked feet hanging off, their sandals on the ground below them, the inevitable umbrella by their side. Most of the village was asleep in nakedness. The color of flesh glowed in the hot shade; brown and sallow in the men, ruddy on the breasts of the women and the entirely nude bodies of the children.

And here, now, we said good-by to the *basha*, and got into the two-wheeled baby wagon, which they call a *kuruma*. One man ran between the shafts, and another, in front, was fastened to the cross-bar by a long strip of cloth tied about

25

him. The file of our five wagons started off at a rapid trot—
we had two for our baggage—with the Doctor ahead, his
white helmet dancing before us in the sun. From under my
umbrella I tried to study and occasionally to draw the
motions of the muscles of our runners, for most of them were
naked, except for the complicated strip around the loins—a
slight development of the early fig-leaf. The vague recall of
the antique that is dear to artists—the distinctly rigid
muscles of the legs and thighs, the rippling swelling of the
backs—revived the excitement of professional study and
seemed a god-send to a painter. The broad, curved hat, lifted
by a pad over the head, was but an Eastern variation, not so
far removed from the Greek πέτασος of Athenian riders.
Some heads were bare; that is to say, their thick black thatch
was bound with a long handkerchief, which otherwise hung
on the shoulders or danced around their necks. Not all were
naked. The youngest, a handsome fellow, had his tunic pulled
up above the thighs, and the slope of his drapery and his
wide sleeves gave him all the elegance of a medieval page. I
found it easier now to struggle against heat and indolence,
and to make my studies as our runners ran along, for we had
entered again the avenue of the great cryptomeria. We had
passed the entrance of another, which in old times was the
road traveled by the Mikado's ambassador, in the fifth
month, when he journeyed across the island to carry
offerings to Iyéyasŭ, in his tomb at Nikko. The big trees
grew still taller in this higher air, their enormous roots
spreading along the embankments in great horizontal lines and
stages of buttresses. Prolonged wafts of cool air blew upon us
from the west, to which we were hurrying. Above us spread a
long avenue of shade, high up and pale in the blue. And so
we got into Nikko as the sun was setting with the delicious
sensation that at last we were in coolness and in shade.

*

Right before us, crossing the setting sun, was the island mountain of Nikko-san; small enough to be taken in by the eye, as it stood framed by greater mountains, which were almost lost in the glittering of wet sunlight. The mountain threw its shade on the little village; down its one long street we rode to the bridge that spans the torrent, which, joining another stream, gives Nikko the look of an island. Alongside this bridge, at a distance of two hundred feet, crosses the red lacquer bridge, over which we are not allowed to pass. It is reserved for the family Tokugawa, the former shoguns of Japan, whose ancestors built the great shrines of Nikko, and for the Emperor on his occasional visits. It stands supported on a gigantic framework of stone, imitating wood, the uprights being pierced to allow the crosspieces to run through, against all European constructional principles, but with a beauty which is Japanese, and a fitness proved by time.

These great posts under the bridge lean against what seems the wall of the mountain; the rock foundation being supplemented, everywhere that a break occurs, by artificial work. Here and there cascades fall over natural and over artificial walls and glisten far up through the trees on the opposite side of the bridge. As we rattled over it, we looked down on the overflowing long wooden trough, which carried the pure waters of the mountain to the village that we had passed, and upon the torrent below, whose limpid clearness was made blue by mist, where the warmer air was chilled by a coldness drawn from far-up mountains. Before us steps of enormous width passed under the foliage and turned above in many directions, and there on the lowest step, her dainty feet on straw sandals, whose straps divided the toes of the close-fitting Japanese socks, with bare ankles, stood our hostess, in latest European dress, most graceful contrast to our own consciousness of being jaded and dirty, and to the nakedness of our runners. Panting with the last run, they stood at rest, and leaned forward against the cross-bar of the shafts, with muscles still trembling, clear streams of sweat varnishing their bronze nakedness, and every hair plastered with wet on forehead, chest, and body. Just before them rustled the unrumpled starched spread of the skirts of the fair American. She was summering at Nikko, and, friendly with the Buddhist clergy, had arranged that one of the priests should let us have his house, and kindly walked with us to it, a little way up in one of the first open spaces of the mountain. After passing the great outside fringe of trees we found a large clear opening, broken up by walled inclosures, the wall sometimes high and sometimes low, and edged by gutters through which the torrents ran. These were the former residences of princes, whom etiquette obliged to worship officially at Nikko. A quarter of a mile up we came to our own garden,— with an enormous wide wall or embankment of stone, some twenty feet deep,—which also had been a prince's, and now belongs to the little Buddhist priest who is our landlord. There are two houses in the inclosure, one of which he lets to us. Ours is brand-new and two stories high, while his is old and low, with an enormous roof, and an arbor built out from the eaves and connecting with his little garden. High behind his house rise rocks and wall; and on top of them are planted willows, pines, maples, and the paulownia, whose broad leaves are part of the imperial crest. A little waterfall tumbles over the rocks and gives us water for our garden and for our bath. In our house we made the acquaintance of Kato, who is to wait upon us. A few minutes later we were welcomed by our landlord, dressed for the occasion. He conducted us to our rooms, and, leaving for a moment, returned with a china bowl that was covered with a napkin, and contained sweetmeats which he told me are peculiar to Nikko.

Seeing that we were helpless with the language, he bowed low and left us to our bath, and to a survey of our new quarters. We were tired, sick, miserable, weary travelers, having gone through a shipwreck of heat and fatigue, but there was a fascination in feeling that this baby-house was ours, that it was typical, that on entering we left our shoes out on our own threshold and were walking on the soft clean mats, stocking-toed; that in a few minutes we should be stretched on these as on a bed, and that Kato would pour out our tea. Our lowest story, which had a veranda, can be divided so as to make a servant's room and a hall beyond. In an L behind stretches out a wash-room with a big dresser fixed to the wall, under which, through a trough, rolls a torrent from the waterfall; and, farther on, is the little square bath-room with one side all open to the floor, when the wooden screen is drawn, through which we get light and air, and through which the box containing burning charcoal is brought from the priest's house to heat our bath. We have a little staircase—just the width of our trunk—which leads sharply up to the veranda above, from which we step into A——'s room and then into mine; they are separated by movable screens, so that we can be about as private as if the division were a chalk line. But outside we have a wealth of moving wall: first the paper screens, which, when we wish, can separate us from the veranda; then, lastly, on its edge, the *amado*, or wooden sliding-doors, which are lying now in their corner box, but which later will be pulled out and linked together, and close the open house for the night.

Then, as we were about leaving, we solemnly placed a great ornamental revolver before the little god of Contentment who sits upon the Tokonoma—that mantelpiece which is at the level of my eye when I lie on the floor, and which is the Japanese ideal seat of honor, but never occupied. This revolver is left there to a appease a Japanese conventional fear of robbers. We went down in the twilight to our friends, and had a very European supper, and sat on their veranda, looking through the trees toward the bridge, in a moonlight of mother-of-pearl; and we were so sleepy that I can only suppose we must have talked of home, and I can only remember our host clapping his hands for lanterns, and Kato leading us back, with the light held low, and the noise of the torrents running under the little stone bridges that we passed, and our taking off our shoes on our own doorstep, and the thunder of the *amado* as Kato rolled them out for the night.

THE SHRINES OF IYÉYASŬ AND IYÉMITSŬ
IN THE HOLY MOUNTAIN OF NIKKO

FROM where we are in the Holy Mountain, our first visit would be naturally to the shrine of the shogun Iyéyasŭ, whose extreme walls I see among the highest trees whenever I look from our balcony over our little waterfall.

Iyéyasŭ died in 1616, having fought, he said, ninety battles and eighteen times escaped death, having almost destroyed Christianity, and leaving his family established as rulers of Japan. In obedience to his dying wishes, his son and successor removed the body of his father from its resting-place in the south to this final tomb at Nikko. Here, in 1617, with complicated and mystic ceremonial, he was buried and deified.

If you have no work on Japan near by to refer to, *sub voce* Iyéyasŭ, I can tell you, briefly, what he did or what he was, though I, too, have no books at my hand. He was a great man, a patient waiter upon opportunity, who at the end of the sixteenth century came upon the scene of a great civil war, then filled by two protagonists, the military ruler, Nobunaga, and his lieutenant, Hidéyoshi, who was to be known later as Taiko Sama. Their aim was to settle something more definitely, of course in their favor; and, in fact, the death of the former and the triumphant success of the latter, who succeeded him, went far toward disposing of many contending claims, and toward a crystallizing of the feudal system, which had grown of centuries of civil war. This is the moment that we see reflected in the annals of the first

Christian missionaries, to whom the military chiefs of Japan were alternately kind or cruel.

When Hidéyoshi died he had grown to be the master of Japan; he had been made Regent of the Empire, as a title of honor, for he was that, and more in reality; he had become one of the greatest of Oriental warriors, and had begun life as a groom, the son of a humble peasant. The name of Taiko (Great Gate) he took like other regents, on retiring nominally from office, but with the addition of Sama (Lord) it is applied to him alone in popular memory. Naturally, then, he believed in a possible dynasty originating in him. At his death he could see, as his greatest fear for the future of the young son to whom he wished to leave his power, this man Iyéyasŭ Tokugawa, lord now of many provinces, but who had begun humbly, and who had assisted him in breaking many enemies, receiving a reward with every success, and consolidating meanwhile his own smaller powers. The dying Taiko made complicated arrangements to secure the good-will of Iyéyasŭ, and also to prevent his encroachments. These arrangements, including and combining the agencies of numbers of princes and vassals, many of them newly Christianized, seem only the more certainly to have forced on a position in which Iyéyasŭ, with few allies, but with clear aims and interests, took the field against a larger number of princes, commanding more men, but not united in any intention as fixed as his was. These he defeated for once and all on a great battlefield, Sékigahara, on some day in October in the year 1600. It was the greatest battle that Japan ever saw, and one of the bloodiest—remarkable for us because of the death of three of the Christian leaders against Iyéyasŭ, warriors distinguished before in many wars, who could not, being Christians, take their own lives in defeat, as their Japanese traditions of honor commanded. Hence the victor had them beheaded—a shameful death, and thereby heroic. These were almost his only immediate victims. Iyéyasŭ wisely forgave, when it paid, and merely weakened the beaten, increasing the possessions but not the powers of his adherents; and finally remained in undisputed power, with great titles from the Mikado, who, though poor in power, was still a dispenser of honors, for, as with the greater gods, the *victrix causa* pleased.

Meanwhile the protection of the son of the great Taiko Sama, for which all this war had been supposed to grow, had not been effected, and even this one obstacle or reminder was to disappear from before Iyéyasŭ, but not for several years, and only just before his death.

He had, in Japanese custom, resigned his apparent power to his son, for behind him he could act more obscurely and with less friction. Then began the drama of the extinction of Christianity; slowly, for many reasons, not the least being that several Christian princes, with their vassals, had supported Iyéyasŭ in his struggle. And at length the son of Taiko Sama, Hidéyori, indirectly connected with the Christian side, fell before Iyéyasŭ. His strong castle at Osaka was said to have become a place of refuge for the persecuted and the discontented, even to the very Christians whom his father had cruelly persecuted.

Which was in the wrong and disturbed the waters, the wolf or the lamb, I do not know, but only that in June, 1615, the great castle was attacked by Iyéyasŭ and his son in as bloody a battle as was ever fought; and notwithstanding that for a moment victory hung in the balance, the Tokugawa Luck prevailed, the castle took fire, thousands perished, and Hidéyori and his mother disappeared.

Whether Iyéyasŭ was the author of the code of laws or rules at which he is supposed to have worked during these years of waiting, with the aid of learned scholars, to bequeath them to his descendants for the maintenance of the order of

33

things he left, I do not know; nor perhaps was the information I once had about them at all accurate. They, or their spirit, however, served to guide the nation for the next two hundred and fifty years; that is to say, until the second Commodore Perry came to Japan, with the increased weight of an outside world much changed.

Meanwhile the great man died, leaving a great personal fame behind him, over and above the powers he could transmit. He was buried here, as I said. The place was chosen in 1616; at the end of the same year the buildings were begun, and in the beginning of the next year were partly completed. When the funeral procession arrived, in nineteen days from Iyéyasǔ's former resting-place, amid great ceremonies and religious rites, the title of "Supreme Highness, Lord of the East, Great Incarnation," was given to the hero and ruler and son of the small laird of Matsudaira.

While he was being thus deified the persecution of the Christians increased in violence, passing into a hideous delirium of cruelty; wiping out its victims, but unable to affect their courage. There can be apparently no exaggeration of the sufferings of the martyrs nor of the strength of mind shown by them—a courage and constancy ennobling to Japan.

Hidetada, the son of Iyéyasǔ, is buried at Yeddo (Tokio); but Iyémitsǔ, the grandson, has a temple and a tomb here in the forest, alongside of his grandfather's.

He succeeded to power in 1623, and lived and ruled some thirty years more with an energy worthy of Iyéyasǔ, and carried the system to completion. The laws known as the laws of Iyéyasǔ are sometimes made out to be his. These laws, based on the old feudal habits, and influenced and directed by the great Chinese doctrines of relationship and duties, are not laws as we think of law, nor were they to be published. They were to be kept secret for the use of the

34

Tokugawa house; to serve as rules for conduct in using their power, so as to secure justice, which is in return to secure power, that exists for its own end in the mind of rulers. These laws, some of which are reflections, or moral maxims, or references to the great man's experience, made out a sort of criminal code,—the relations of the classes,—matters of rank and etiquette, and a mechanism of government. They asserted the supremacy, and at the same time destroyed the power, of the Mikado, and by strict rules of succession, residence, and continued possession bound up the feudal nobles. They reasserted the great individual virtues of filial piety and of feudal loyalty, and insisted on the traditions of military honor. "The sword" was to be "the soul of the Samurai," [1] and with it these have carried the national honor and intelligence in its peculair expressions.

Full recognition was given to the teaching, "Thou shalt not lie beneath the same sky, nor tread on the same earth, with the murderer of thy lord." The rights of the avenger of blood were admitted, even though he should pay the penalty of his life.

Suicide, which had long been a Japanese development of chivalrous feeling and military honor, was still to be regarded as purifying of all stain, and, for the first time, allowed in mitigation of the death penalty.

Indeed, half a century later, the forty-seven Ronin ("wave-people"—Samurai who had lost their natural lord and their rights) were to die in glorious suicide, carrying out the feudal idea of fidelity.

You know the story probably; at any rate, you will find it in Mitford's tales of old Japan. It is a beautiful story, full of noble details, telling how, by the mean contrivance of a certain lord, the Prince of Ako was put in the wrong, and his

[1] The Samurai, the entire warrior class of the feudal days; therefore, also, the gentry.

35

condemnation to death and confiscation obtained. And how, then, forty-seven gentlemen, faithful vassals of the dead lord, swore to avenge the honor of their master, and for that purpose to put aside all that might stand in the way. For this end they put aside all else they cared for, even wife and children, and through every obstacle pursued their plan up to the favorable moment when they surprised, on a winter night, in his palace, among his guards, the object of their vengeance, whose suspicions had been allayed by long delay. And how his decapitated head was placed by them upon his victim's tomb, before the forty-seven surrendered themselves to justice, and were allowed to commit suicide by hara-kiri, and how they have since lived forever in memory of Japan.

These laws, then, destroyed nothing; they reasserted certain Japanese traditions and customs, but made out, through many details, the relations of dependence of all classes of society upon the shogun, as vassal indeed of the Mikado, but supreme ruler who held the key of all. All this did Iyémitsŭ carry out, as well as the consequent seclusion of the country; the only manner of avoiding ideals which might clash with those upon which this consolidation of the past was based. And to many of these ideals, to the idea of the sacredness of the family, to the idea of subjection to the law of the ruler, Christianity, by its ideal of marriage, by its distinctions of the duty to Cæsar,—to name only a few reasons,—might be found an insidious dissolvment. Therefore, if it be necessary to find a high motive, Iyémitsŭ did what he could to trample out the remains of Christianity, which were to expire, a few years after his death, in a final holocaust as terrible and glorious as Nero himself could have wished to see.

From that time, for two centuries, all went on the same, until the arrival of the foreigners found a system so complete, so interlocked and rigid, as to go to pieces with the breaking of a few links.

That break was supplied by the necessity of yielding to the Christian and foreign demand of entrance, and in so far abandoning the old ways.

With this proof of weakness the enemies of the Tokugawa and those of the system began to assert themselves, circumstances aiding, and in 1868 the last of the race resigned all powers and retired to private life.

The details of the enormous changes, as they followed one another, are too many and sudden, and apparently too contradictory, for me to explain further. Even now I repeat this deficient summary of the Tokugawa story only because of wishing to recall who they were that have temples and tombs about us, and to recall, also, that such has been the end of the beginning which is buried here.

The approach to the temple, to which most paths lead, is through a great broad avenue, a quarter of a mile long, bordered by high stone walls, above which rise high banks and higher trees. Between these dark green walls, all in their own shade,—in the center of the enormous path and in the full light of the sky,—a brilliant torrent rushes down in a groove of granite, hidden occasionally under the road. Here and there drop out from the walls noisy columns of clearest water.

In the distance beyond, through a mass of closer shade, made by two rows of dark cryptomeria, that are planted on banks faced with stones,—for here the road divides into three different grades of ascent by enormous steps,—shine the high white walls of the temple grounds, edged with a red-lacquered fence and a black roofed gate of red and gold. In the open space before it, with wide roads diverging through high walls, crowned with scarlet fences, stands a granite

Torii, some thirty feet high, whose transverse stones are crossed by a great black tablet, marked with the gilded divine name of Iyéyasŭ. On one side a five-storied pagoda, graceful and tall, certainly one hundred feet high, blood-red and gold in the sunlight, and green, white, and gold in the shadows of its five rows of eaves, rises free from the trees around it and sends a tall spear, encircled with nine gilded rings, into the unbroken sky. Bindings and edges of copper, bright green with weathering, sparkle on its black roofs, and from their twenty corners hang bells of bright green copper. Above the steep steps, against the white wall, we pass through the first gate. It is recessed, and two gigantic columns of trees stand in the corners. Two monsters of uncertain lion-form occupy the niches on each side. From the upper side of the red pillars, as supports for the engaged lintel, stretch out the gilded heads of tapirs,—protectors against pestilence,—of lions and elephants, and great bunches of the petals of the peony. Above, the architrave and frieze are painted flat with many colors and with gold, and the ends of the many beams which support the roofing are gilded. Everywhere, even to the ends of the bronze tiles of the black roof, the crest of Iyéyasŭ's family, the Tokugawa, is stamped in gilded metal.

At the inside corner of the gate stands a gigantic cedar, said to have grown to this height since the time when Iyéyasŭ carried it about with him in his palanquin. Opposite to three red buildings, which are storehouses for the memorial treasures of the temple, stands, closer to the wall, a charming building, mostly gray,—partly owing to the wearing of the black lacquer with time,—and decorated with carved panels, which make a frieze or string-course all around its sides. Above this line of green, red, blue, white, and gold, a large space of gray wood, spotted with gilt metal where the framework of the outer beams is joined, spreads up to the pediment under the eaves, which is all carved and painted in a ground of green. The heavy roof above is of black bronze and gilded metal and is spotted with the golden Tokugawa crest. Below the colored band, midway, the black wall has gratings with golden hinges, for this delicate splendor is given to a stable— the stable of the sacred horse of the god Iyéyasŭ. The patient little cream-colored pony has no look of carrying such honors; and I can scarcely imagine his little form galloping out in the silence of the night under the terrible rider.

A gentle splashing of water, which mingles with the rustling of the trees and the quiet echoes of the pavement, comes from the end of the court where its edge is a descent filled with high forest trees. This lapping sound comes from the temple font, a great wet mass of stone, looking like solid water. It has been so exactly balanced on its base that the clear mountain stream overflows its sides and top in a perfectly fitting liquid sheet. This sacred well-basin has a canopy with great black bronze-and-gold roof, supported by white stone pillars, three on each corner, that are set in bronze sockets and strapped with gilded metal. The pediment and the brackets which cap the pillars are brilliantly painted, and the recessed space below the curved roof-beam is filled with palm-like curves of carved waves and winged dragons. Next to this, and at right angles to it, is a heavy bronze Torii, through which we go up to another court, turning away from the buildings we have seen. On the dark surface of the Torii glisten the golden Tokugawa crests; on the great tie-beam, the upper pillars, and the central upright. Near us, the eaves of its lower roof continuing the lines of the water-tank pavilion, is the closed library, red, delicately adorned with color under the eaves, and with the same heavy black roofing of bronze dotted with gold which all the buildings have in a heavy monotony. The steps lead us to another court, spotted with different buildings, among tremendous trees—a bronze pavilion with a hanging bell, a bell tower, and a drum tower, closed in with sloping walls of red lacquer, and a large lantern of bronze under a bronze pavilion, whose curious, European, semi-Gothic details contrast suddenly with all this alien art, and prove its origin a tribute from trading Christian Holland to the mortal deity worshiped here. On one side, where the forest slopes down in sun and shadow, stands a Buddhist temple, sole survivor of the faith in this place, now turned over to the official and native worship. The latticed gold-and-black screens were all closed, except in the center, through which we could see the haze and occasional glitter of the gold of gods and altar ornaments, and the paleness of the mats. On its red veranda stood a young Buddhist priest, whom our companions knew; a slight, elegant figure, a type of modesty and refinement. Farther back, on the other side of the veranda, an older companion looked down the valley at some girls whose voices we could hear among the trees.

The main entrance rises above the high steps to a little esplanade with heavy railing, on the level of a higher embankment. The court that we were in was full of broken shadows from its own tall trees, and from all this accumulation of buildings, red-lacquered and gilded, black-and-bronze roofed, spotted and stained with moss and lichens, or glittering here and there in their many metals. Long lines of light trickled down the gray trunks and made a light gray haze over all these miscellaneous treasures. Great lanterns (toto) of stone, capped with green and yellow moss, metal ones of bronze and iron, stand in files together here and in the lower court, or are disposed in rows along the great stone wall, which is streaked by the weather and spotted with white and purple lichens. Along its upper edge runs the red-lacquered wall, heavily roofed, of the cloister which surrounds the farther court above. Its face is paneled between the metal-fastened beams and posts with two rows of deep carvings of innumerable birds and trees and waves and clouds and flowers. All these are painted and gilded, as are the frieze above and the intervals between the gilded rafters.

On all this space, and on the great white gate, the "Gate Magnificent," the full sun embroidered the red and white and colored surfaces with millions of stitches of light and shadow.

The gate, or triumphal arch, is a two-storied building with heavy bronze-tiled roof, capped and edged, like all the rest, with gilded metal, and spotted with the gilded crest of the Tokugawa. Its front toward us rises in the well-known curve, shadowing a pediment, full of painted sculpture. Eight white pillars embroidered with delicate reliefs support the white lintel, which is embossed with great divine monsters and strapped with gilded metal. In the niches on each side are seated two repellant painted images, inside of white walls, which are trellises of deeply-carved floral ornament. These figures are warriors on guard, in ancient and Japanese costume, armed with bows and quivers of arrows, whose white, wrinkled, and crafty faces look no welcome to the intruder, and recall the cruel, doubtful look of the guardian statues of foxes that protect the entrances of the primitive shrines of the land-god Inari. The far-projecting white capitals are the half-bodies of lion-like monsters with open mouths and stretched-out paws. Above these, below the carved balcony which marks the second story, the cornice is made of a wilderness of tenfold brackets, black lacquered and patterned with gold, and from each of the ten highest ones a gilded lion's head frowns with narrowed eyes.

The balcony is one long set of panels—of little panels carved and painted in its white line with children playing among flowers. Above, again, as many white pillars as below; along their sides a wild fringe of ramping dragons and the pointed leaves of the bamboo. This time the pillars are crowned with the fabulous dragon-horse, with gilded hoofs dropping into air, and lengthy processes of horns receding far back into the upper bracketings of the roof. Upon the center of the white-and-gold lintel, so delicately carved with waves as to seem smooth in this delirium of sculpture, is stretched between two of the monster capitals a great white dragon with gilded claws and gigantic protruding head. But all these beasts are tame if compared with the wild army of dragons that cover and people the innumerable brackets which make the cornice and support the complicated rafters under the roof. Tier upon tier hang farther and farther out, like some great mass of vampires about to fall. They are gilded; their jaws are lacquered red far down into their throats, against which their white teeth glitter. Far into the shade spreads a nightmare of frowning eyebrows, and pointed fangs and outstretched claws extended toward the intruder. It would be terrible did not one feel the coldness of the unbelieving imagination which perhaps merely copied these duplicates of earlier terrors.

So it is, at least, in this bright, reasonable morning light; but I can fancy that late in autumn evenings, or in winter moonlight, or lighted by dubious torches, one might believe in the threats of these blinking eyes and grinning jaws, and fear that the golden terrors might cease clinging to the golden beams. It is steadying to the eye to meet at last the plain gold-and-black checker pattern of the ends of the final rafters below the roof, and to see against the sky peaceful bells like inverted tulips, with gilded clappers for pistils, hanging from the corners of the great bronze roof.

And as we pass through the gate we are made to see how ill omen was turned from the Luck of the Tokugawa by an "evil-averting pillar," which has its pattern carved upside down as a sacrifice of otherwise finished perfection.

I noticed also that a childish realism has furnished the lower monsters of the gate with real bristles for their distended nostrils; and this trifle recalls again the taint of the unbelieving imagination, which insists upon small points of truth as a sort of legal protection for its failing in the greater ones.

Within this third cloistered court which we now entered is an inclosed terrace, some fifty yards square. Inside of its walls are the oratory and the final shrine, to which we can pass through another smaller gate, this time with lower steps. The base of the terrace, which makes the level of the innermost court, is cased with large blocks of cemented stone. Above it is a fence or wall with heavy roof and projecting gilded rafters. Great black brackets support the roof. Between them all is carved and colored in birds and flowers and leaves, almost real in the shadow. Between the decorated stringcourses the wall is pierced with gilded screens, through which play the lights and darks, the colors and the gilding of the shrine inside. At the very bottom, touching the stone plinth, carved and painted sculptures in high relief project and cast the shadows of leaves and birds upon the brilliant granite.

Beyond this inclosure and the shrine within it the court is abruptly ended by a lofty stone wall, high as the temple roof, and built into the face of the mountain. From its very edge the great slope is covered with tall trees that look down upon this basin filled with gilding and lacquers, with carvings and bronze, with all that is most artificial, delicate, labored, and transitory in the art of man.

It is in this contrast, insisted upon with consummate skill, that lies the secret beauty of the art of the men who did all this. The very lavishness of finish and of detail, the heaped-up exaggerations of refinement and civilization, bring out the more the simplicity and quiet of the nature about them. Up to the very edges of the carvings and the lacquers grow the lichens and mosses and small things of the forest. The gilded temples stand hidden in everlasting hills and trees,

43

open above to the upper sky which lights them, and to the changing weather with which their meaning changes. Nothing could recall more completely the lessons of death, the permanence of change, and the transitoriness of man.

We went up the steps of the recessed gate, which repeats the former theme of white and gold and black in forms of an elegance that touches the limits of good taste. Its heavy black roof, whose four ridges are crowned by long bronze dragons and crawling lions, opens in a high curve on the front and sides to show under the bent white-and-gold ridge-beams a pediment strapped and intersected by spaces of small carvings, white and tinted, relieved by red perpendiculars of beams.

White and gold shine in the great brackets and the recesses of the rafters. Below the white frieze, carved with many small figures of Chinese story, the pillars and the lintel are inlaid in many carved woods, ornaments of dragons, plants, and diapered patterns on the whitened ground. The opened doors repeat the same faint tones of wood, and of white and gold, and of gilded metals. The walls, which are open at the base, are merely lattice screens. Their exquisite flowered patterns fluctuate with gilded accents of whites, greens, lavenders, and blues.

The gate inside is, therefore, nothing but an ornamented trellis, made still lighter by contrast with the solid white doors, trellised at top, but whose lower panels are exquisitely embellished with inlaid carved woods and chiseled golden metal. We took off our shoes, and ascended the bronze-covered steps of the oratory and shrine, which come down from the red-lacquered veranda, behind the four carved white pillars of the descending porch. Great white dragons with spiky claws project from the pillars, and crawl in and out of the double transom. In the shadow of the roof golden monsters hang from the complex brackets. The friezes and bands of the temple face are filled with carving, delicate as embossed tapestry, while the panels, deeply cut into auspicious forms of birds and flowers, carry full color and gold far up into the golden rafters.

All recesses and openings are filled with half-realities, as if to suggest a dread or a delicious interior, as flowers might pass through palings, or great beasts, types of power, might show great limbs through confining barriers. The long building, indeed, is a great framework, strongly marked, dropped on a solid base, and weighted down by a heavy roofing. The white pillars or posts which divide its face and corners stand clear between the black-and-gold latticed screens, partly lifted, which make almost all its wall.

Strips of the sacramental white paper hang from the lower lintel against the golden shade of the interior. Inside, pale mats cover the black-lacquer floor. Exquisite plain gold pillars, recalling Egyptian shapes, divide the gilded central walls. Here and there on the gilded tie-beams curved lines of emerald-green or crimson, like tendrils, mark with exquisite sobriety a few chamfered cuttings. On either side of the long room (fifty feet) are two recesses with large gold panels on which symbolic forms are freely sketched, and carved inlays of emblematic birds fill their farthest walls. Their ceilings are carved, inlaid, and painted with imperial flowers, mystic birds, and flying figures, and the pervading crest of the Tokugawa. For these were the waiting-rooms of the family, and, as A—— remarked, the impression is that of a princess's exquisite apartment, as if the Tartar tent had grown into greater fixity, and had been touched by a fairy's wand.

All was bare except for an occasional sacred mirror, or hanging gilded ornament, or the hanging papers of the native worship; and this absence of the Buddhist images and implements of worship left clear and distinct the sense of a personal residence—the residence of a divinized spirit, not unlike the one that he was used to in life.

Even more, on the outside of the building the curved stone base, like a great pedestal, with pierced niches filled with flowers carved and painted between the great brackets that support the veranda, makes the temple seem as if only deposited for a time, however long that time may be.

We merely looked at the central passage, that, dividing the building, leads down and then up to the shrine itself, and waited for the time when we shall get further permission, and I shall be allowed to sketch and photograph. As for me, I was wearied with the pleasure of the endless detail; for even now, with all my talk, I have been able to note but a little of what I can remember.

We withdrew, put on our shoes again at the gate, and turned below to the east side of the court. We passed the Hall of Perfumes, where incense was once burned while the monks chanted prayers in the court, as they did when Iyéyasŭ was buried. We passed the Hall of the Sacred Dances, whose open front makes a large, shady, dim stage, with a great red railing on its projecting edge. Within it moved a white shadow, the figure of a woman-dancer. And then we came to a white-and-gold gate, inside of the roofed cloister wall. Above the open door that leads to it sleeps a carved white cat, in high relief, said to have been the work of a famous left-handed sculptor, carpenter, and architect. Its cautious rest may not have been so far from the habits of the living Iyéyasŭ, to whose tomb, farther on, this is the entrance.

Framed by the gold and white of the gate and of the half-opened door rise the steps built into the hillside and all carpeted with brilliant green mosses. The stone railings, which for two hundred feet higher up accompany the steps, are also cushioned with this green velvet, and our steps were as noiseless as if those of the white cat herself. All is green, the dark trees descending in sunlight to our right and rising on the bank to our left, until we reach an open space above, with a bank of rocky wall inclosing the clearing.

Here is the small final shrine, and behind it a stone esplanade with a stone fence, within which stands, in the extreme of costly simplicity, the bronze tomb of Iyéyasŭ. A large bronze gate, roofed in bronze, of apparently a single casting, with bronze doors, closes the entrance. Before the monument, on a low stone table, are the Buddhist ornaments—the storks, the lotus, and the lion-covered vases, all of brass and of great size.

The tomb itself is of pale golden bronze, in form like an Indian shrine: a domed cylinder surmounted by a great projecting roof which rises from a necking that separates and connects them above—the roof a finial in the shape of a forked flame. Five bronze steps, or bases, support this emblematic combination of the cube, the cylinder, and the globe.

The crest of the Tokugawa, ten times repeated, seals the door upon the burnt ashes of the man who crystallized the past of his country for more than centuries, and left Japan as Perry found it. All his precautions, all his elaborate political conservatism, have been scattered to the winds with the Luck of the Tokugawa, and the hated foreigner leans in sightseeing curiosity upon the railing of his tomb.

But the solemnity of the resting-place cannot be broken. It lies apart from all associations of history, in this extreme of cost and of refined simplicity, in face of the surrounding powers of nature. There is here no defiance of time, no apparent attempt at an equal permanency; it is like a courteous acceptance of the eternal peace, the eternal nothingness of the tomb.

We leaned against the stone rails and talked of Iyéyasŭ— of his good nature, of his habit of chatting after battle, of his

47

fraudulent pretensions to great descent; and of the deadening influence of the Tokugawa rule, of its belittling the classes whose energies were the true life of the country. We recognized, indeed, that the rulers of Iyéyasǔ's time might have perceived the dangers of change for so impressionable a race, but none of us asked whether the loss of hundreds of thousands of lives of courageous Christians had been made up in the strength of the remaining blood.

Far away the sounds of pilgrims' clogs echoed from the steps of distant temples; we heard the running of many waters. Above us a few crows, frequenters of temples, spotted the light for a moment, and their cries faded with them through the branches. A great, heavy, ugly caterpillar crept along the mossy edge of the balustrade, like the fresh incarnation of a soul which had to begin it all anew.

IYÉMITSŬ

WE were told by our good friends that the temple of Iyémitsŭ; the grandson of Iyéyasŭ, far less pretentious than the shrine of the grandfather and founder, would show us less of the defects which accompanied our enjoyment of yesterday. The successors of Iyémitsŭ were patrons of art, sybarites, of those born to enjoy what their ancestors have sown. The end of the seventeenth century has a peculiar turn with us, a something of show and decadence, of luxury and want of morals; and the same marks belong to it even in Japan. Indeed, I feel in all the Tokugawa splendor something not very old, something which reminds me that this was but the day of my own great-grandfather; a time of rest after turmoil, of established sovereigns on various scales, of full-bottomed wigs, of great courtliness, of great expenses in big and little Versailles. I miss the sense of antiquity, except as all true art connects with the past, as the Greek has explained when he said that the Parthenon looked old the moment it was done.

. . . .

The temple of Iyémitsŭ is, indeed, charming and of feminine beauty, complete, fitted into the shape of the mountain like jewels in a setting. From near the red pagoda of Iyéyasŭ's grounds a wide avenue leads, all in shade, to an opening, narrowed up at its end to a wall and gate, which merely seem a natural entrance between the hills. There are great walls to the avenue, which are embankments of the mountains. From them at intervals fountains splash into the torrents at each side, and overhead are the great trees and their thin vault of blue shade. The first gate is the usual roofed one, red, with gilded rafters and heavy black bronze tiles, and with two red muscular giants in the niches of the sides. Its relative simplicity accentuates the loveliness of the first long court, which we enter on its narrowest side. Its borders seem all natural, made of nothing but the steep mountain sides, filled with varieties of leafage and the columns of the great cedars. These indeterminate edges give it the look of a valley shut at each end by the gate we have passed, and by another far off disguised by trees. This dell is paved in part, and with hidden care laid out with smaller trees. Down the steep hillside, a cascade trembles through emerald grass, part lost, part found again, from some place where, indistinct among the trees, the jaws of a great bronze dragon discharge its first waters. A simple trough collects one rill and sends it into the large stone cube of a tank, which it brims over and then disappears.

The little pavilion over this well is the only building in the inclosure. It is more elegant than that of Iyéyasŭ, with its twelve columns, three at each corner, sloping in more decidedly, their white stone shafts socketed in metal below and filleted with metal above, melting into the carved white architrave. In the same way the carvings and the blue and green and red and violet of the entablature melt in the reflections under the shadow of the heavy black-and-gold roof with four gables. From under the ceiling, and hanging below the lintels, flutter many colored and patterned squares of cloth, memorials of recent pilgrims.

As we turn to the highest side of the court on the left and ascend slowly steep, high steps to a gorgeous red gate above our heads, whose base we cannot see, the great cedars of the opposite side are the real monuments, and the little water-tank, upon which we now look down, seems nothing but a little altar at the foot of the mountain forest. The gate, when we look back, is only a frame, and its upper step only a balcony from which to look at the high picture of trees in shadow and sunlight across the narrow dell which we can only just feel beneath us.

The great red gate has two giant guardians of red and green, and innumerable bracketings for a cornice, all outlined, and confused all the more by stripes of red and green and white and blue.

Just behind the gate, as if it led to nothing, rises again the wall of the mountain; then we turn at right angles toward a great esplanade, lost at its edges in trees, from which again the forest would be all the picture were it not that farther back upon the hill rises a high wall, with a platform and lofty steps, and the carved red-and-gold face of a cloister, with another still richer gate of a red lacquer, whose suffering by time has made it more rosy, more flower-like.

Up these steps we went, the distant trees of the mountains ascending with us, and we rested in the red-and-gold shade. Above us the gold brackets of the roof were reflected back, in light and dark, upon the gold architrave, adorned by the great carved peonies, red and white, and great green leaves which stood out with deep undercutting. From the fluted red columns projected great golden tapirs' heads and paws, streaked with red like the bloom of tulips. The gilded metal sockets and joinings and the faint modeled reliefs of the wall, all of dull gold, looked green against the red lacquer. Beyond, the inner lintel was green, like malachite, against the sunny green of the forest. Its chamfered edge reflected in gold the lights and shadows beyond, and against the same green trees stood out the long heads and trunks of the tapir capitals in red and gold.

Through this framework of red and many-colored gold we passed into the inner court, made into a cloister by walls and

51

narrow buildings, rich in red lacquer and black and gold. As before with Iyéyasŭ, so also within this inclosure, is another raised upon a base faced with great blocks of granite, fretted, spotted, and splashed with white and purple lichens. The sun-embroidered wall or fence that edges it is black with a bronze-and-gold roof; its trellises are of white, edged with gold; as usual, bands of carved and colored ornament divide so as almost to pierce its face; and its beams are capped with jointings of chiseled metal. The central gate spots joyously the long line of black and gold and color and bronze, with imposts of white carving, framed in rosy lacquer, and with gold pillars and a gold lintel, upon which is spread a great white dragon, and with a high gold pediment, divided by recesses of golden ornament on ultramarine, and with golden doors fretted with a fairy filagree of golden ornament.

Through this lovely gate, with an exquisite inlaid ceiling of pearl and gold and walls of carved and colored trellises, we pass to the main shrine, only just behind it.

Here again, less pretense than with Iyéyasŭ, and greater and more thoughtful elegance. The long white carved columns of the portico run straight up to the brackets of its roof—except where, to support the cross-beam of the transoms, project red lions' heads and paws, looking like great coral buds. The entire architrave of the building is divided into a succession of long friezes, stepping farther and farther out, like a cornice, until they meet the golden roof. Only a few gold brackets support the highest golden beam— carvings, color, and delicate stampings of the lacquer embroider the gold with a bloom of color. The gold doors look like jewelers' work in heavy filagree.

All within was quiet, in a golden splendor. Through the small openings of the black-and-gold gratings a faint light from below left all the golden interior in a summer shade, within which glittered on lacquer tables the golden utensils of the Buddhist ceremonial. From the coffered ceiling hangs the metal baldachin, like a precious lantern's chain without a lamp.

The faces of the priests who were there were known to us, the elder's anxious and earnest, the younger's recalling an Italian monsignore. One of them was reading by the uplifted grating and rose to greet us, and to help to explain. We entered the narrow passage which makes the center, through whose returning walls project, in a curious refinement of invention, the golden eaves of the inner building beyond. Gratings which were carved and gilded trellises of exquisite design gave a cool, uncertain light. We passed out of a trellised door on to the black lacquered floor of a veranda and then sat awhile in a simple room with our hosts to look at temple manuscripts and treasures, and at the open palanquin which once brought here the dead Iyémitsŭ—not reduced to ashes, as his grandfather Iyéyasŭ, but wrapped and covered up in innumerable layers of costly and preserving vermilion. We passed into the corridor behind the building and looked at the picture hanging on the wall, which faces the mountain and the tomb, in which Kuwan-on the Compassionate sits in contemplation beside the descending stream of life. Then for a few moments we entered by a low door the sanctuary, narrow and high and with pyramidal roof.

By the flickering torch which alone gave light, all seemed of gold—the wall, the columns which run up to the central golden roof, and the transoms which connect them. In the darker shade stood a golden shrine, never opened. Whatever precious details there may be were bathed in a shade made of reflected gold. An exquisite feeling of gentle solemnity filled the place. We passed out suddenly into the glare of day and under the blazing blue sky, which hung over the inclosure of tall trees and the temple like the ceiling of a tent.

Again a great wall, spotted with moss and lichens, is built

around as an inclosure. It makes a base for the greater wall of the mountain rising above it, which is covered with forest trees, as if the skirting of the wilderness of northern Japan were here suddenly limited. Across one single opening, on the one side, where show the seams of the immense cyclopean construction, and joining two corners, broken by great patches of the shadows of the gigantic trees, stretches a white wall, heavily roofed, against a shadow almost black. In its center is a strange, white gate-building, moundlike in shape, absolutely plain, but capped by a great roof, which is stretched out upon a mass of brackets, all gold and colors, and with carved golden doors, whose central panels are all fretted and chiseled and stamped with the Wheel of the law. Here begin the distant steps leading through the trees to the tomb where lies the body of Iyémitsŭ, cased in layers of vermilion, under golden bronze, like his grandfather Iyéyasŭ, and surrounded by the still more solitary splendor of the forest.

Astonishing as is the contrast to-day, in the abundance and glory of summer, of the bronze and the lacquered colors, and the golden carvings, with the wild rocks and trees, the grass and the mosses, I should like to see in the snow of winter this richness and glitter and warmth of red and white and black and gold.

Can it bring out still more the lavishness of refinement, which wells up as if exhaustless? Does its white monotony and the dark of the great cedars make one feel still more the recklessness of this accumulation of gold and lacquer and carving and bronze, all as if unprotected and trusted to the chances of the recurring seasons?

As we repeat each look, on our slow return through the temples, the same elegance, the same refinement, the same indifference to the outrages of time, contrast again with the permanence and the forces of nature. With the fatigue and

54

repetition of the innumerable beauties of gold and color, carving and bronze, the sense of an exquisite art brings the indefinable sadness that belongs to it, a feeling of humility and of the nothingness of man. Nowhere can this teaching be clearer than in this place of the tombs. It is as if they said, serenely or splendidly, in color and carving and bronze and gold: "We are the end of the limits of human endeavor. Beyond us begins the other world, and we, indeed, shall surely pass away, but thou remainest, O Eternal Beauty!"

TAO: THE WAY

OSOMI and Tategawa were the architects of Nikko; Osomi planned the lovely pagoda, — so I am told, — and I hasten to put down their names. At that time the great Tenkai was abbot. He was a friend and adviser of Iyéyasŭ, as he was the teacher of Iyémitsŭ, the grandson, and of Hidetada, the less illustrious son. It may be with him that Iyéyasŭ arranged the plan of fixed endowment for the Church; and endowment not to be added to or diminished, so that it should be an element of stability and no longer a fluctuating danger. With this seems to have ended the possible reasons for military dependents in the service of the Church.

Tenkai is said to have planned or prepared beforehand the temples of Iyéyasŭ, which might explain the extremely short time given in the record for their buildings; so that, begun in 1616, the stable, the surrounding edifices, and the shrine were completed in the third month of 1617.

I have been careful to give you some account of the temples of Iyéyasŭ and Iyémitsŭ, because I regret having said so little of those temples of Shiba in Tokio, where the remainder of the Tokugawa rulers repose in a state adorned by similar splendors. But these temples of the founders are of a more complete type, and, with one exception, seem to me more impressive. Yet even with the beauties that I have tried to describe, I am still not quite so carried away as I might have been by such complete works of art. There is a something, a seeming of pretense or effort or ingeniousness, which I

56

cannot seize, but which seems to me to belong to a splendor not quite secure, or perhaps only just secured,—something like what I might call the mark of the parvenu.

Yes; I think that is it. It is still, after all this time, just a little new. But what thorough adaptation of means to ends; how delicately subtle the arrangements, and simple; and how impossible to describe through words or drawings. How the result alone is aimed at, and what little parade is made of the intention and preparation. This work, which seems to betray an inferiority to its own ideal—this work, which has even a touch of the vulgar, is charming enough to look like a fairyland. It displays a capacity for arrangement which none of us to-day could hope to control; has a charm that any passer-by could feel; has more details of beauty than all our architects now living, all together, could dream of accomplishing in the longest life. When I began to reflect how this wood and plaster had more of the dignity of art and of its accessible beauty than all that we have at home, if melted together, would result in; that these frail materials conveyed to the mind more of the eternal than our granite, it seemed to me that something was absolutely wrong with us.

And the cause of this result was not the splendor of line and color; it was not the refinement. The last time I could recall a similar sensation had been before some little church tower of England; it was certainly the subordination of all means to a single end, and their disappearance in one impression.

. . . Since my first visit to the temples my mind has been dwelling more and more in an involuntary manner upon the contrast with all modern art, and I venture to note down for you some of the thoughts forced upon me. It seems as if I were really reminded of what I always knew, or ought to have known; and perhaps what I may say about ourselves is as good a way as any other of giving an opinion upon what I see here. For, indeed, what I see here that I admire I feel as though I had always known, had already seen; it is rather most of our own that seems queer, strange, and often unreasonable.

I can make no set and orderly arrangement of my rather confused thinking, but can only trace it out as it occurred to me—as if it were from outside; as if something whispered to me now and then out of small occurrences, and said, "Don't you understand more clearly?"

... On leaving the temples we went back to our friend's house, which was once the residence of the regent of Japan— a large, low wooden building of the kind so carefully described by Mr. Morse in his book. All is extremely simple; there is nothing to call any attention. The woodwork is merely put together with great care; some little panels of the closets are nicely trimmed with metal and highly ornamented. This, with metal nail-heads and a pretty wall-paper, is all the decoration.

Here we found the mail and papers, and enjoyed the watering-place feeling of news from town. There were copies of "Life" and of the London "Punch," many of whose drawings did not look out of place in this land of clever sketchers. Indeed, that in them which once seemed good across the seas still held its own in presence of the little prodigies of technique that one meets in Japanese drawings.

Indeed, they recalled one another. Both call out one's sudden recollection of some facts in nature; and besides, all good sketches resemble one another as being the nearest approach to the highest finished work. They have in common with it the essential merit of being better than they appear, of indicating more than is necessary to tell the tale, of not being strictly measurable quantities. We grow so ungrateful when too well treated that we forget how Mr. Du Maurier throws in, over and above the social epigram in lines, an elegance and grace that might belong to a poetic picture; that Mr. Keene tells his story over and over again in the very folds of each individual's dress; that he will, unconcernedly, present us with a landscape as full of nature as his human figures, instead of the indifferent background which would have been sufficient for the story of the caricaturist. Now, the feeling of disenchantment, of having "found out" appearances, of having come to the end of a thing, is never forgiven by the average healthy mind. In greater things one turns, some day, to those which are always richer and fuller of meaning with time,—as one looks to-day at a Corot or a Delacroix or a Millet once uncared-for,—and that means that at length our eyes are opened. The sketch, like the great work of art, is better than it appears, and recalls to me the emperor in the story, whom the old woman could not recognize in the presence of the big drum-major. We can appreciate what suffering the little old woman underwent when she discovered her mistake, and how she never forgave the big drum-major. For mankind has never believed at heart that the work itself is to be judged, but has always (at least in the case of one's neighbor) acknowledged that it is the *work of art which judges us*.

So says a Japanese friend, and I think that he has it exactly. Hence an importance attaches to criticism which otherwise would be inexplainable,—the importance there is in being right,—because we shall be judged ourselves if we are wrong, and often by ourselves as judges.

. . . And late numbers of the magazines had come, pleasant to look over before dinner,—while the noiseless servants glided over the matting, and our hostess put on her Japanese costume,—serving to make the distance greater, as we feel that all goes on at home with the usual regularity.

Some architectural sketches in facsimile in a magazine

became entangled with the thread of my thinking and brought to my mind an inevitable lesson.

They were charming, and so different from the realities which they were meant to embody. One I dwelt upon, bright and clever, where every dark of window or of shadow intensified the joyfulness of the white wall of a residence at home, which you daily pass. In the reality, alas! its Fifth Avenue monotony is unrelieved. The wall is not bright, the windows are paler than the walls, and the projections and adornment are duller yet. The drawing was an abstraction, probably meant for the sweet enticement of the client, and was what the building *should have been*. The draughtsman "knew better than he builded." As my mind analyzed this curious professional misstatement of truth, it seemed to me that I could see how the art of architecture in Japan was real compared to ours, even though none of their architects, any more than those of the great past of the world, could have made such a drawing—such a brilliant promise of a performance not to be, such a beautifully engraved check upon a bank where there were no funds. Not knowing the science and art of perspective drawing, not the power of representing shadows according to rule, nor having the habit of ruling lines with a ruler to give interest, nor of throwing little witty accents of dark to fill up blanks, they were perhaps the more obliged to concentrate their powers upon the end of the work; and their real motive was the work itself.

This may be strange and contradictory to the modern Western mind, gradually accustomed to polished cartoons for bad paintings and worse glass, to remarkable designs for decoration and architecture which look their best in wood-cuts, to great decorative paintings which are carried out so that they may be photographed without any injury to their color, nay, to its vast improvement. Do you remember how

B——, the famous sculptor, used to preach to me that to-day no one looked at a thing itself, no one expected to, and that the fame of the artist was for those whose work could be adequately represented in the newspapers. That an excellence which could not be duplicated, that a tone which could not be matched, that a line which could not be copied, was not to be appreciated and could not be cared for. In fact, that such refinements were only worthy of the mind of an Oriental, "of a man accustomed to wear the moon embroidered on his back." Why spend days in obtaining the color of a wall which any architect will think can be adequately replaced by his description of something like it to the painting firm around the corner? Why make the thing itself, if something like it will do as well? Why strike the note exactly, if any sound near it satisfies the average ear? For us, to-day, things and realities no longer exist. It is in their descriptions that we believe. Even in most cultivated France an architect or designer like Viollet-le-Duc will seriously undertake to restore old work, every square inch of which had had the patient toil of souls full of love and desire of the best, by rubbing it all out, and making a paper drawing or literary description for others to restore again in a few modern weeks the value of ancient years of ineffably intelligent care. Consider this impossibility of getting a decent restoration carried out by our best intelligences, and note that while they are unable with all money and talk and book-learning to replace the past in a way that can deceive us, there exist patient, obscure workmen who, beginning at the other end of the work, produce little marvels of deception in false antiquities—purchased by museums and amateurs for sums their authors never could get in their proper name. But these latter have only one object, the thing itself, and are judged by the result; while we, the arbiters and directors better known, who never employ them, are satisfied, and satisfy others by our having

61

fled in the archives of to-day notices that we are going to do something in the utterly correct way. I took as an example our friend Viollet-le-Duc, the remarkable architect whose works we have both studied, because he had written well,— in some ways, no one more acutely and more wisely; because of his real learning, and on account of his very great experience. Is all that this man and his pupils did in their own art of making, worth, as art, the broken carving that I kick to-day out of my path?

Has such a risible calamity ever occurred before in any age? Destruction there has been, replacing of old, good work with better or with worse by people who did not understand, or care, or pretend to care; but the replacing of good with bad by people who do understand, and who claim to care, has never been a curse until to-day. This failure in all restoration, in all doing of the thing itself, must be directly connected with our pedantic education and with our belief in convenient appliances, in propositions, in labor-saving classifications, in action of paper, in projects for future work, in soul-saving theories and beliefs—in anything except being saved by the—work itself.

Indeed, I have always felt that perhaps in the case of poor Richardson, just dead, we may begin to see the shape of an exception, and can realize what can be accomplished through what we called deficiencies. He was obliged, in the first place, to throw overboard in dealing with new problems all his educational recipes learned in other countries. Then, do you think that if he had drawn charming drawings beforehand he would have been able to change them, to keep his building in hand, as so much plastic material? No; the very tenacity needed for carrying out anything large would have forced him to respect his own wish once finally expressed, while the careful studies of his assistants were only a ground to inquire into, and, lastly, to choose from.

For many little prettinesses and perfections do not make a great unity. Through my mind passes the reminiscence of something I have just been reading, the words of an old Chinese writer, an expounder of Tao (the Way), who said what he thought of such matters some twenty-five centuries ago. What he said runs somewhat in this way:

The snake hissed at the wind, saying: "I at least have a form, but you are neither this nor that, and you blow roughly through the world, blustering from the seas of the north to the seas of the south."

"It is true," replied the wind, "that I blow roughly, as you say, and that I am inferior to those that point or kick at me, in that I cannot do the same to them. On the other hand, I blow strongly and fill the air, and I can break huge trees and destroy large buildings. *Out of many small things in which I do not excel I make* ONE GREAT ONE *in which I do excel.*"

In the domains of the One there may not be managing.

Hence, also, the difficulty, I had almost said the impossiblity, of finding a designer to-day capable of making a *monument:* say, for instance, a tomb, or a commemorative, ideal building—a cathedral, or a little memorial. There is no *necessity* in such forms of art, nothing to call into play the energies devoted to usefulness, to getting on, to adaptation, to cleverness, which the same Taoist says is the way of man, while integrity is the way of God.

Art alone, pure, by itself, can be here the object of the maker's contemplation; the laws of the universe that men call beauty are the true and only sufficient materials of construction.

With what preparation does a designer of humbugs come to such work, failure in which cannot be excused because of any practical reasons, because of any pressing necessities—

that really belongs to the public, to everybody more than to its possessor, or to its owner, or to those who have paid for it—that, finally, can be saved from adverse criticism only for a short time, while passing interests are concerned.

Who knows this better than yourself? Where on earth to-day can you find a thing done by us designers that an artist will go to look at for love, for the deep desire of enjoyment which makes us visit so many little things of the past, and go far for them? If you can, imagine any painter desiring to note, so as to make them his own by copy, a modern set of moldings, the corner of a modern building.

And yet what a rush of delight comes upon us with a few Greek moldings, with a fragment of Greek or Gothic ornament, with the mere look of the walls of some good old building. How the pleasure and the emotions of those who made them have been built into them, and are reflected back to us, like the smile from a human face. I know that I have told you often how the fragment of a Gothic window from old English Boston set into the cloister of Trinity of the new Boston always seemed to me to outweigh the entire building in which it rests. And yet it is only a poor fragment of no great period. But then the makers thought and felt in the materials that they worked in, even if their drawings were rude and incomplete and often incorrect. And no architect seems to realize to-day that his walls could give us the same emotions that we receive from a Rembrandt, or a Van Eyck, or a Veronese, and for the same reasons, and through a similar use of a real technique.

You draw well; you can make a sketch, I am sure, which, like many others, would have spots of light on a black surface, or a pretty wash of sky above it, or little patches of shadow, like clever lichens, spread over it, and that would be correct in artificial perspective, and recall something of older design, and have no great blemishes to take hold of. How far would it help you to have made a million such if you seriously wished to do a thing for itself, not for its effects upon a client, nor for a claim upon the public, nor for a salve to your own vanity?

And now do you see how, as we architects and designers gradually work more and more on paper and not in the real, our energies are worked out in accomplishing before we get to our real work,—that of *building* a *work of art*,—and the result of our drawing grows feebler and feebler and tamer as it presses to its end. Then, for this weak frame of conception, the men who have come in to help (and that only because the director's time would not admit of his doing all himself, otherwise he would, in his jealous weakness, adorn as poorly as he imagines)—then, I say, if the painter, the sculptor, the decorator, shows any strength or power, there is another danger. There is danger that the sculptor's relief will be more powerful than the weak projections of solid masonry,—that the line of the painter will be grander and more ample than those which were meant to guide and confine them—that the paint of the decorator will appear more massive and more supporting than the walls of the architect. Whence all will be tamed, all annulled and made worthless and paltry, so as not to disturb the weak efforts of the master directing. And for the first time in the history of art we shall have buildings which the Greek or the Roman, the Medieval or the Oriental, would have been unable to adorn, while in their times the masters who were architects, great and small, found no trouble in placing within their buildings, made famous to all time by this choice, the sculptures of the Parthenon or of Olympia, the glass or the statues of Christian cathedrals, or the carvings of India or of Japan.

So that when the greatest painter of the century left instructions for his tomb, he asked that it should be copied

65

from some former one of antiquity or renaissance, so that it might have—to typify his love and his dislikes—masculine moldings and a manly character, contrary, as he said, "to all that is done to-day in architecture."

You may say that through all this wandering of thought I am telling you little about Japanese art. Wait; perhaps I may be merely preparing your mind and mine for what I shall have to say later. Or, rather, let us think that I am carried away by the spirit, and that I am certainly talking of what I do not find here; and if there is no novelty in what I say, and that you know it, and have always known it, we shall come back to what you also know, that art is the same everywhere and always, and that I need not come this distance to learn its principles. If there is anything good here, it must resemble some of the good that we have with us. But here at least I am freer, delivered from a world of canting phrases, of perverted thought, which I am obliged to breathe in at home so as to be stained by them. Whatever pedantry may be here, I have not had to live with it, and I bear no responsibility in its existence. And then again, art here seems to be a common possession, has not been apparently separated from the masses, from the original feeling of mankind.

To-day at dinner, Kato, who was waiting upon us, could give his opinion upon the authenticity of some old master's work, at the request of our host, himself a great authority; so that I could continue my dreaming through the conversation and the semi-European courses, marked by my first acquaintance with the taste of bamboo shoots—a little delicacy sent in by A-chin, the children's nurse.

Much was talked of the Tokugawa race, and some cruelty was shown to their memory as a family of parvenus who had usurped the power theoretically invested in the mikados— an usurpation practised over and over again by every successful shogun, as by Yoritomo, Taikosama. Indeed, the

Ashikaga move through Japanese history against a background of mikados. And when O——comes in later he talks of Masashige, and of others, who during centuries, at long intervals, attmepted to realize what has now been accomplished—the restoration of the mikado to his ancient powers and rulership of twenty centuries ago.

Yes, the Tokugawa splendor was that of parvenus. Their half-divine masters lie in no gilded shrines nor under monumental bronze, but buried beneath the elements, their graves marked only by mounds or trees, as it might have been with their earliest ancestors, the peaceful chieftains of a primitive family: a simplicity recalled to-day by the little fragment of dried fish that accompanies presents, in memory of the original humility of the fishing tribes, the ancestors of this almost over-cultivated race.

These Tokugawa, then, were parvenus, and naturally asked of art, which lasts and has lasted and is to last, an affirmation of their new departure. This splendor was made for them, and its delicious refinement has not quite escaped that something which troubled me at Shiba—an anxiety that all should be splendid and perfect, an unwillingness to take anything for granted. And yet, by comparison, this looks like a fairyland of refinement. What should we do when called to help a new man to assist or to sweeten his acquired position? What vulgarity of vulgarities should we produce? Think of the preposterous dwellings, the vulgar adornments given to the rich; the second-hand clothing in which newly acquired power is wrapped. The English cad, and the Frenchman not good enough for home, put the finishing touch upon the proofs of culture which are to represent them to their children.

I need not refer to what is seen in San Francisco as an example. At home in New York we have more than are pleasant to think of. I know that some may say that we have only

67

what we deserve for thinking that we can escape, in the laws that govern art, the rules that we have found to hold in everything else.

Some years ago I told you how once a purveyor of decorations for the millionaire, a great man in his line, explained to me how and why he had met his clients half-way. "You despise my work," he said, "though you are too polite so say so," — for we were friendly in a manner, — "and yet I can say that I am more thoroughly in the right than those who would seek to give these men an artistic clothing fit for princes. Is there anything more certain than that the artist represents his age, and is all the greater for embodying it. Now that is what I do. You will say that my work is not deeply considered, though it is extremely careful in execution; that its aims are not high; that it is loud occasionally—when it is not tame; that it shows for all it is worth, and is never better than it looks. And who, pray, are the people that live surrounded by what I make? Are they not represented by what I do? Do they not want show of such a kind as can be easily understood, refinement that shall not remind others of a refinement greater than theirs, money spent largely, but showing for every dollar? They want everything quick, because they have always been in a hurry; they want it on time, whatever happens, because they are accustomed to time bargains; they want it advertisable, because they live by advertising; and they gradually believe in the value of the pretenses they have made to others. They are not troubled by what they feel is transient, because their experience has been to pass on to others the things they preferred not to keep. They feel suspicious of anything that claims or seems to be better than it looks; is not their business to sell dearer than they buy? They must not be singular, because they must fit into some place already occupied.

"I claim to have fully expressed all this of them in what I

do, and I care little for the envious contempt of the architects who have to employ me and who would like to have my place and wield my influence. And so I reflect my clients, and my art will have given what they are."

Thus the great German rolled out his mind with the Teutonic delight at giving an appearance of pure intellect to the interested working of his will—incidentally sneering at the peacock feathers, the sad-eyed dados, the poverty-stricken sentimentality, half esthetic, half shopkeeper, of his English rivals, or at the blunders in art which Mr. Stanford White once called our "native Hottentot style."

Of course my German was merely using a current sophistry that is only worth quoting to emphasize the truth.

Augustus, the greatest of all parvenus, did not ask of Virgil to recall in verse the cruelties of civil war. No true artist has ever sought to be degraded; no worker of the Middle Ages has reflected the brutality of the world around him. On the contrary, he has appealed to its chivalry and its religion. No treacherous adventurer of the Renaissance is pictured in the sunny, refined architecture that was made for him. You and I know that art is not the attempt at reflecting others, at taking possession of others, who belong to themselves; but that it is an attempt at keeping possession of one's self. It is often a protest at what is displeasing and mean about us; it is an appeal to what is better. That is its most real value. It is an appeal to peace in time of brutal war, an appeal to courageous war in time of ignoble peace; it is an appeal to the permanent reality in presence of the transient; it is an attempt to rest for a moment in the true way.

We are augurs conversing together, and we can afford to laugh at any respected absurdity. We know that cleverness is not *the way* to the reality; cleverness is only man's weak substitute for integrity, which is from God.

All these words—miscalled ideas—poured out by my

German friend and his congeners are merely records of merchants' ways of looking at the use of a thing, not at the thing itself. Such people are persuaded that they must surely know about the thing they sell or furnish. If not they, then who? For none can be so impartial, as none are so disinterested, in the use of the thing sold.

It is too far back for you to remember the charming Blanco, the great slave-dealer, but you may have heard of his saying, which covers the side of the dealer. He had been asked why he felt so secure in his judgment of his fellow-creatures, and especially of women. "Because," said he, "I have traded in so many"—*J'en ai tant vendu.* I have sometimes quoted this saying to dealers in works of art, to dealers in knowledge about art, without, however, any success in pleasing them. In fact, one has no judgment of one's own in regard to anything sold that is not a matter of utility until one feels quite thoroughly, as if it were one's own, the sense of Talleyrand's treatment of the persuasive dealer. I am sure that you do not know the story. Two friends of his, ladies of rank, had chosen his study as a place of meeting. They wished to select some ring, some bracelet, for a gift, and the great jeweler of Paris was to send one of his salesmen with sufficient to choose from. Of course the choice was soon limited to two, and there paused, until Talleyrand, sitting at the farther end of the long library, called out, "Let me undertake to help you to make your decision. Young man, of these two trinkets tell me which you prefer." "This one, certainly, your Excellency." "Then," ended the experienced cynic, "please accept it for your sweetheart; and I think, ladies, that you had better take the other." I tell you anecdotes; are they not as good as reasons?

Listen to what my Chinese writer says: "Of language put into other people's mouths, nine-tenths will succeed. Of language based upon weighty authority, seven-tenths. But language which flows constantly over, as from a full goblet, is in accord with God. When language is put into other people's mouths, outside support is sought. Just as a father does not negotiate his son's marriage, for any praise he could bestow would not have the same value as praise by an outsider. Thus the fault is not mine, but that of others, who would not believe me as the original speaker." Again, a story of China comes back to me, told by the same writer, who lived before our purer era, and who was, as a Japanese friend remarks, a strategist in thought, fond of side attacks, of presenting some point apparently anecdotic and unimportant, which, once listened to, turns the truthful mind into channels of fresh inquiry. The anecodote is old, told by the old writer many centuries before Christ, and before any reflections about art troubled our barbarian minds.

It is about a court architect who flourished in celebrity some twenty-seven centuries ago, and who answered admiring queries as to how he did such wonderful things. "There is nothing supernatural about it," he said. "I first free my mind and preserve my vitality—my dependence upon God. Then, after a few days, the question of how much money I shall make disappears; a few more days, and I forget fame and the court whose architect I am; another day or so, and I think only of THE THING ITSELF. Then I am ready to go into the forest"—the architect and the carpenter were one then—"whose wood must contain the form I shall seek. As you see, there is nothing supernatural about it."

Twenty-seven centuries ago the formula of all good work was the same as it has been since. This looking for "the thing itself," not for the formula to control it, enabled men who were great and men who were little, far down towards us, far down into the times of the Renaissance (until pedantry and night covered human freedom and integrity), to be painters or poets, sculptors or architects, as the occasion required, to the astonishment of our narrowed, specialized vision of the last two hundred years.

Again, if I have not put it clearly enough in this story of the far East, let me add another, which includes the meaning of the first. You will forgive it in honor of the *genius loci*, for these writings of the Chinese philosophers form a staple of conversation and discussion in social gatherings of cultivated people here. The story is of the greatest of Chinese rulers, the "Yellow Emperor" of some forty-seven centuries ago. He was in pursuit of that law of things, that sufficient ideal which is called "Tao" ("the Way"), and he sought it in the wilds beyond the world known of China, in the fabulous mountains of Chu-tzu. He was accompanied by Ch'ang Yu and Chang Jo, and others of whom I know nothing; and Fang Ming, of whom I nothing also, was their charioteer. When they had reached the outside wilderness these seven sages lost their way. By and by they fell in with a boy who was tending horses, and they asked him if he knew the Chu-tzu Mountains. "I do," said the boy. "And can you tell us," said the sages, "where Tao, the law, abides?" "I can," replied the boy. "This is strange," said the Yellow Emperor. "Pray tell me how would you govern the empire?"

"I should govern the empire," replied the boy, "in the same way that I tend my horses. What else should I do? When I was a little boy and lived within the points of the compass my eyes grew dim. An old man advised me to visit the wilderness outside of the world. My sight is now better, and I continue to dwell outside of the points of the compass. I should govern the empire in the same way. What else should I do?"

Said the Yellow Emperor, "Government is not your trade, but I should be glad to learn what you would do." The boy refused to answer, but being urged again, said: "What difference is there between governing the empire and looking after horses? See that no harm comes to the horses; that is all."

Thereupon the emperor prostrated himself before the boy; and calling him divine teacher, took his leave.

I am writing these vagaries by the sound of the waterfall in our garden; half of the *amados* are closed; the paper screens near me I have left open, and the moths and insects of the night flutter around my lamp in orbits as uncertain as the direction of my thoughts. I have given up my drawing; it is too hot to work. And I have already tired myself with looking over prints and designs. Among them there is a sketch by Hokusai which reminds me of the way in which my mind bestrides stray fancies that float past. The picture is that of Tekkai (the beggar), the Sennin exhaling his spiritual essence in a shadowy form, which shadow itself often rides away upon the spirit horse that Chokwaro or Tsuga evokes occasionally from his traveling-gourd.

To-day we talked of the legends of these Rishi or Sennin, whose pictures so often come up in the works of Japanese artists.

Rishi or Sennin are beings who enjoy rest,—that is to say, are exempt from transmigration,—often in the solitude of mountains for thousands of years, after which delay they again enter the circle of change. If they are merely human, as many of them are, they have obtained this charm of immortality, which forms an important point in the superstitious beliefs and practices of modern Taoism. These appear to have no hold in Japan, as they have in China, but these personages, evolutions of Taoist thought, live here at least in legend and in art.

The original mysticism from which they sprung is full of beauty and of power. General Tcheng-ki-tong has recently stated it well, when he says that Lao Tzŭ, its great antique propounder, speaks with the tone of a prophet. He neither preached nor discussed, yet those who went to him empty departed full. He taught the doctrine which does not find expression in words, the doctrine of Tao, or the Way—a doctrine that becomes untrue and uprofitable when placed in set forms and bound in by pedantry, but which allows teaching by parables and side glimpses and innuendoes as long as they are illuminated by that light which exists in the natural heart of man. And I, too, am pleased to let myself be guided by this light. After many years of wilful energy, of forced battle that I have not shunned, I like to try the freshness of the springs, to see if new impressions come as they once did in childhood. With you I am safe in stating what has come to me from outside. It has come; hence it is true: I did not make it. I can say with the Shadow, personified by my expounder of the Way,[1] that when the light of the fire or the sun appears, then I come forth; when the night comes, I lie still: I wait indeed, even as they wait. They come and I come, they go and I go too. The shade waits for the body and for the light to appear, and all things which rise and wait wait upon the Lord, who alone waits for nothing, needs nothing, and without whom things can neither rise nor set. The radiance of the landscape illuminates my room; the landscape does not come within. I have become as a blank to be filled. I employ my mind as a mirror; it grasps nothing, it refuses nothing; it receives, but does not keep. And thus I can triumph over things without injury to myself—I am safe in Tao.

[1] Prémare's "Notitia Linguæ Sinicæ," "4um exemplum. Sic inducit Tchouang-tsee umbram loquentem: Ego quidem existo, sed nescio qua ratione. Ego sum veluti cicadarum tunicæ et Serpentis spolia," etc. If what I have written is ever seen by H. B. M.'s consul at Tamsui, he will perceive my present indebtedness to his most admirable translations.

JAPANESE ARCHITECTURE

I FEAR that of all my description the refrain of the works gold and bronze will be all that you will retain. How can I have any confidence in my account of anything so alien, whose analysis involves the necessary misuse of our terms, based upon another past in art?—for words in such cases are only explanations or easy mnemonics of a previous sight. But soon I shall have photographs to send, and if I can summon courage for work, in this extreme heat and moisture, I shall make some drawings. But again, these would not give the essential reasons for things being as they are; and whatever strange beauties would be noted, they might appear to have happened, if I may so say, and not to have grown of necessity. It is so difficult for our average way of accepting things to think of what is called architecture without expecting structures of stone—something solid and evidently time-defying.

And yet, if architecture represents the needs of living of a people, the differences that we see here will have the same reasonableness that other devices show elsewhere. The extreme heat, the sudden torrents of rain, will explain the far-projecting and curved roofs, the galleries and verandas, the arrangements for opening or closing the sides of buildings by sliding screens, which allow an adjustment to the heat or the damp. But weightier reasons than all these must have directed in the construction of such great buildings as the temples, and I think that, putting aside important race influences, these sufficient reasons will be found in the volcanic nature of Japan and its frequent earthquakes. Whatever was to be built must have had to meet these difficult problems: how successfully in the past is shown by a persistence of their buildings which to us seems extraordinary, for many of them are lasting yet in integrity for now over a thousand years.

I speak of the influences of race, because it is evident that very many traditions, prejudices, and symbolic meanings are built into these forms, and that many of them must have come through the teachings of China. Everywhere the higher architecture, embodied in shrines and temples, is based on some ideal needs, and not essentially upon necessities; is, in fact, a record or expression of a religious idea or mystery. In this case I am too profoundly ignorant, as most of us are, to work out origins; but my mind feels the suggestion of an indefinite past, that once had meanings and teachings, just as my eye recognizes in the shape of the massive temples the image of a sacred box, or ark, once to be carried from place to place. There is, perhaps, in this direction a line of study for the men to come.

Like all true art, the architecture of Japan has found in the necessities imposed upon it the motives for realizing beauty, and has adorned the means by which it has conquered the difficulties to be surmounted. Hence no foundations, which would compromise the super-imposed building by making it participate in the shock given to its base. Hence solid pedestals, if I may so call them, or great bases, upon which are placed only, not built in, the posts which support the edifice, leaving a space between this base and the horizontal beams or floors of the building. The building is thus rendered elastic, and resumes its place after the trembling of the earthquake, and the waters of bad weather can escape without flooding any foundations.

The great, heavy, curved roof, far overhanging, weighs down this structure, and keeps it straight. An apparently unreasonable quantity of adjusted timber and beams supports the ceiling and the roof. Complicated, tremendous corbelings, brackets grooved and dovetailed, fill the cornices as with a network; but all these play an important practical part, and keep the whole construction elastic, as their many small divisions spread the shock.

Still more, in such a building as the charming pagoda at Iyéyasŭ's shrine, which is full one hundred feet high, slight-looking and lithe, the great beam or mast which makes its center does not support from the base, but is cut off at the foundation; and hence it acts as a sort of pendulum, its great weight below retarding the movement above when the earthquake comes.

I have heard the whisper of a legend saying that the architect who devised this, to correct the errors of a rival and partner, was poisoned in due time, in jealous return. For those were happy times when backbiting among artists took the more manly form of poisoning.

Now besides all this, which gives only the reason for the make of certain parts which together form the unity of a single building, there are other prinicples before us. The relation of man to nature, so peculiarly made out in the Japanese beliefs, is made significant, symbolized, or typified through the manner in which these buildings are disposed. A temple is not a single unity, as with us, its own beginning and end. A temple is an arrangement of shrines and buildings meaningly placed, often, as here, in mountains—a word synonymous with temples; each shrine a statement of some divine attribute, and all these buildings spread with infinite art over large spaces, open, or inclosed by trees and rocks. The buildings are but parts of a whole. They are enveloped by nature, the principle and the adornment of the subtle or mysterious meaning which links them all together.

Besides all this is the religious symbolism underlying or

77

accompanying all, as once with us, of which I know too little to speak, but which can be felt and occasionally detected because of many repetitions. But this would carry me beyond my limits; and, indeed, we find it very difficult to obtain any more information from our instructors, whether they do not know securely, or whether they reserve it for better minds and worthier apprehensions. Nor do I object to this Oriental secrecy or mystery, as it adds the charm of the veil, which is often needed.

And I should wish that soon some one might undertake to make out in full the harmony of proportions which has presided over these buildings. It is evident that a delicate and probably minute system of relations, under the appearance of fantasy, produces here the sense of unity that alone makes one secure of permanent enjoyment. My information on the subject is fragmentary: I know that the elegant columns are in a set relation to the openings of the temple; that the shape of these same columns is in another relation to their exquisite details; that the rafters play an important part, determining the first departure. I have seen carpenter's drawings, with manners of setting out work and measurements, and I feel that there is only a study to carry out.

Nor is my wish mere curiosity, or the interest of the antiquarian. What we need to-day is belief and confidence in similar methods, without which there is nothing for ourselves but a haphazard success; no connection with the eternal and inevitable past, and none with a future, which may change our materials, but will never change our human need for harmony and order.

You have heard of the little gardens, and of their exquisite details, in which the Japanese makes an epitome of nature, arranged as if for one of his microscopic jewels of metals, ivory, or lacquer.

Here in our own garden there would seem no call for an

artificial nature. The mountain slope on which we live must have always been beautiful of itself; but for all that, our garden—that is to say, the space about our landlord's house and our own—has been treated with extreme care. Our inclosure is framed towards the great temple groves, and the great mountains behind them, by a high wall of rock, over which, at a corner edged with moss, rolls a torrent, making a waterfall that breaks three times. The pool below, edged with iris that grow in the garden sand, is crossed by a bridge of three big flat stones, and empties secretly away. On each side of the fall, planted in the rock wall, stands a thick-set paulownia, with great steady leaves, and bending towards it a willow, whose branches drop far below itself and swing perpetually in the draught of the waterfall. Bunches of pink azalea grow in the hollows of the rocks, and their reflections redden the eddies of the pool. Steps which seem natural lead up the wall of rock; old pines grow against it, and our feet pass through their uppermost branches. On the top is planted a monumental stone, and from there a little path runs along, leading nowhere nowadays, as far as I can make out. I am right in calling this mass of rock, which is a spur of the mountain's slope, a wall; for I look down from its top to the next inclosure far below, now overgrown and wild. What is natural and what was made by man has become so blended together, or has always been so, that I can choose to look at it as my mood may be, and feel the repose of nature or enjoy the disposing choice of art.

Where the little bridge crosses over, and where mossy rocks dip down a little to allow a passage, edged by a maple and a pine, I look over across the hidden road to a deserted *yashiki*, with one blasted tree, all overgrown with green and melting into distances of trees which, tier behind tier, reach to a little conical hill, that is divided and subdivided by sheets of mist at every change of heat and damp, so that I feel half as if I knew its forms perfectly—half as if I could never get them all by heart.

In the sand of our little garden are set out clumps of flowers, chrysanthemum mostly, and occasionally iris and azalea; and the two houses make its other two sides. The priest's house, an old one, with large thatched roof projecting in front and supported there by posts covered with creepers, is nearer the water. I see the little priest with his young neophyte curled on the mats in the big front room whose whole face is open; while in a break, or wing, is the opening to the practical housekeeper side of the dwelling.

Our own house, which faces south like the priest's, completes the square, as I said. It is edged on the outside by a small plantation of trees with no character, that stretch away to the back road and to a wall terracing a higher ground behind. There a wide space overgrown with bushes and herbage, that cover former care and beauty, spreads out indefinitely toward conical hills hot in the sun, behind which rises the great volcanic slope of Nio-ho. A little temple shrine, red, white, and gold, stands in this heat of sunlight and makes cooler yet the violets and tender greens of the great slopes. This is to the north. When I look toward the west I see broad spaces broken up by trees, and the corner of Iyéyasŭ's temple wall half hidden by the gigantic cedars, and as I write, late in the afternoon, the blue peak of Nan-tai-san rounded off like a globe by the yellow mist.

The garden, embosomed in this vastness of nature, feels small, as though it were meant to be so. Every part is on a small scale, and needs few hands to keep things in order. We have a little fountain in the middle of the garden, which gives the water for our bath, and sends a noisy stream rolling through the wooden trough of the wash-room. The fountain is made by a bucket placed upon two big stones, set in a basin, along whose edge grow the iris, still in bloom. A hidden pipe fills the bucket, and a long, green bamboo makes a conduit for the water through the wooden side of our house. With another bamboo we tap the water for our bath. In the early morning I sit in the bath-room and paint this little picture through the open side, while A——, upstairs in the veranda, is reading in Dante's "Paradiso," and can see, when he looks up, the great temple roof of the Buddhist Mang-wanji.

Occasionally the good lady who takes care of our priest's house during his weeks of service at the temple of Iyémitsŭ salutes me while at my bath, for the heating of which her servant has supplied the charcoal. She is already dressed for the day, and in her black silk robe walks across the garden to dip her toothbrush in the running water of the cascade. Then in a desultory way she trims the plants and breaks off dead leaves, and later the gardener appears and attends to one thing after another, even climbing up into the old pine tree, taking care of it as he does of the sweet-peas; and I recall the Japanese gardener whom I knew at our Exposition of 1876, as I saw him for the last time, stretched on the ground, fanning the opening leaves of some plant that gave him anxiety.

Thus the Japanese garden can be made of very slight materials, and is occasionally reduced to scarcely anything, even to a little sand and a few stones laid out according to a definite ideal of meaning. A reference to nature, a recall of the general principles of all landscapes,—of a foreground, a distance, and a middle distance; that is to say, a little pic-ture,—is enough. When they cannot deal with the thing itself—when they do, they do it consummately—they have another ideal which is not so much the making of a real thing as the making of a picture of it. Hence the scale can be diminished, without detriment in their eyes, until it becomes lilliputian to ours. All this I take to be an inheritance from

China, modified toward simplicity. I do not know to what type our little garden belongs. For they have in their arrangements manners of expressing ideas of association, drawing them from nature itself, or bringing them out by references to tradition or history, so that I am told that they aim to express delicate meanings which a Western imagination can hardly grasp; types, for instance, conveying the ideas of peace and chastity, quiet old age, connubial happiness, and the sweetness of solitude. Does this make you laugh, or does it touch you—or both? I wish I knew more about it, for I am sure that there is much to say.

I have spoken of simplicity. The domestic architecture is as simple, as transitory, as if it symoblized the life of man. You can see it all in the drawings, in the lacquers, and it has recently been treated completely in the charming book of Professor Morse. Within, the Japanese house is simplicity itself; all is framework, and moving screens instead of wall. No accumulations, no bric-à-brac; any lady's drawing-room with us will contain more odds and ends than all that I have yet seen together in Japan. The reserved place of honor, a sort of niche in the wall, the supposed seat of an ideal guest, has upon its bench some choice image on a stand, or a vase with elegant disposal of flowers or plants, and above it the hanging roll with drawing or inscription. Perhaps some other inscription or verse, or a few words on a tablet upon some cross-beam, and perhaps a small folding screen. Otherwise all works of art are put aside in the fireproof store-house, to be brought out on occasions. The woodwork is as simple as it can be—occasionally, some beautiful joinery; and above all, exquisite cleanliness. For there are no beds—only wadded coverlets and the little wooden pillow, which does not disturb the complicated feminine coiffure in the languors of the night. No tables; food is laid on the cleanly mats, in many trays and dishes. No chairs; the same mats that serve

82

for bedstead and table serve for seats with, perhaps, a cushion added.

And this is all the same for all, from emperor's palace to little tradesman's cottage. There is nothing, apparently, but what is necessary, and refinement in disposing of that. The result is sometimes cold and bare. There is the set look of insisting upon an idea—the idea of doing with little: a noble one, certainly; as, for instance, when the emperor's palace at Kioto is adorned merely by the highest care in workmanship and by the names of the artists who painted the screen walls— in solitary contradiction to the splendor and pomp of all absolute rulers, no storehouse for the wasted money of the people, but an example of the economy which should attend the life of the ruler. It is possible that when I return I shall feel still more distaste for the barbarous accumulations in our houses, and recall the far more civilized emptiness persisted in by the more esthetic race.

BRIC-À-BRAC

I NEED not tell you that the pervading manner of spending time and money is always within our reach. We do not go after the owner and seller of bric-à-brac; he comes to us.

Coming from afar,—from Tokio, a hundred miles away, and from Ozaka, four times that distance,—bales of merchandise are unloaded at our door, or at our friends' for us. Patient pack-horses stand in the inclosure of the yards; big parcels, and piles of boxes and bundles, encumber the verandas. Weary hours, beginning with excitement and ending with gentle disappointment, are spent in indecision of judgment and uncertainty of purchase. But there remains always at the bottom of the boxes a delusive hope, and some treasure may perhaps reward our patience.

And then, besides occasional beauties in color or design, there is something in looking over all these débris of civilization in their own home; and odds and ends, having not much more excuse for themselves than that they remain, help to explain either the art of the habits of the country, or its history, or the nature we see about us. We have found almost nothing among the things brought us which can rank as work of high art, and I am afraid that we must be looked down upon by our friends for purchases which have no excuse in any lofty esthetic code. But they have the charm of being there, and of explaining, and in another way of teaching, even when they are bad, and often because they are bad. Because their very poverty helps to a classification and to an

84

analysis of the means through which the artist worked, and to a knowledge of the prevalent subjects and arrangements which he found ready to his hand, bequeathed to him by an earlier and nobler choice.

From all this poor stuff exhales the faded scent of a greater art and refinement, which is now invisible, or destroyed, or subsisting only in fragments, difficult of access, or which are far away. And there is a peculiar unity in the arts of the extreme East. We must remember that this very sensitive Japanese race has developed in its art, as in everything, without being subjected to the many direct and contradictory influences which have made our Western art and civilization. There have been here, within historic times, no vast invasions of alien races, bringing other ways for everything in thought and in life, and obliging an already complex civilization to be begun over and over again on readjusted bases; no higher living and advanced thought obliged to yield for times and half times, until the grosser flames of energy could be purified; no dethronement, within society tried by every other calamity, of the old primeval faith. Instead of a tempest of tastes and manners of feeling blowing from every quarter, and in which the cruder dislikes have held for centuries the balance against cultured likings and devotion, Japan has been carried on in one current, in which have mingled, so as to blend, the steady influences of the two most conservative civilizations of India and of China.

All here to-day, and for far back, is interwoven with Chinese thought, breaks through it, returns to it, runs alongside of it. And through Buddhism, its fervor, its capacity for taking up in its course boulders of other creeds or habits, a something different, higher in aspiration and in form, has lived with everything else and affected all.

This impressionable race found, contrasting with and supporting its nature, secure, steady, undeviating guides, so that these foreign ideals have persisted here with a transplanted life. In fact, it is possible to look to Japan to find something of what ancient China was. So much of what has here been done, as their language does to-day, saves for us a hint or a reflection of the great Chinese ages, when China had not yet been conquered by the foreigner, and when energies apparently unknown to the China of to-day flourished with the strength of youth. The art and literature of Japan, therefore, represent in great part the Chinese prototype—an original which for us has practically disappeared. We cannot easily know what arrangements and compositions, what free interpretations of the world, or severe imitations of nature, the old Chinese adopted, but they are reflected or continued in the styles and subjects and treatments of what we call Japanese. The limits and definitions of each may be clear to the Japanese critic, but to our casual Western eye they merge or derive one from the other, like some little-known streams which make one river.

Almost all the arrangements that we know so well on Japanese drawings, screens, bronzes, lacquers, ivories, etc., have Chinese prototypes. And all this is over and above the constant use of Chinese legend, and story, and philosophy, which are to Japan what Greece and Rome used to be to us—a storehouse of associated meanings and examples.

Would it amuse you if I made out some of the types that you see?

Here are the pine-tree and the stork, emblems of long life; or the bamboo and the sparrow, which typify the mildness and gentleness of nature.

The willow waves in the wind to and fro, and the swallows swing forth and back again.

The names of Color and of Love are joined by a similarity of sound, and probably by a mystic association: and so you will see upon the screens that the leaves of the maple turn red in autumn, when the stag calls the doe. The cherry-blossom's splendor is for show, like the pheasant's plumage.

Long centuries ago the plum became the poet's tree, because of an early poet's verses; and the nightingale, also a singer and a poet, is associated with the tree.

The tiger hiding in the jungle has a background of bamboo, as the oxen have the peach-tree, from an old Chinese sentence: "Turn the horse loose on the flower-covered mountain, and the ox into the orchard of peaches."

The cock stands on the unused war-drum, which is a Chinese symbol of good government, the aim of which is peace.

Or, again, legends and stories are referred to.

The cuckoo flies across the crescent of the moon, and the story of Yorimasa is called up, who slew with bow and arrow the mysterious monster that had tormented the life of the Mikado Narihito. I despair of telling the story without great waste of words, and I half-regret having chosen the example; but, perhaps, it is all the more Japanese for its complication.

You must know that the Mikado—this was about the year 1153—had been ill night after night with terrible nightmares, to the confusion of his numerous doctors; and that his many feminine attendants had done all they could to soothe him, to no avail. Every night, at the hour of the Bull (two A.M., an hour when evil power is great), the dovecote was fluttered by this fearful visitation. But, at length, either these gentle dames or other watchers noticed that before each access a cloud had drifted over the palace, and that, resting just above the sleeping-apartments, two lights shone out from the dark mass. Then the bells of the city temples sounded the hour of the Bull. The gentlemen of the palace and the imperial guards were set on watch, the priests prayed to ward off the evil influence; but uselessly. Then Yorimasa—a brave warrior, a famous archer, one of the guards—was allowed, or ordered, to try to destroy the evil thing whatever it might be. He, with a follower, watched nightly until the dark cloud and the shining orbs were near, when the great bow of Yorimasa was discharged, and a strange and wonderful beast fell blinded to the ground.

The sword of Yorimasa despatched it in nine separate blows, and the thing,—said to have had something of the monkey, the tiger, and the serpent,—was burned to ashes. For this Yorimasa was given the girl he loved, the Lady Iris-flower (who, therefore, had not watched in vain), and with her the celebrated sword called Shishino-o (King of Wild Boars). Now the imperial deputy, as he presented this sword to Yorimasa, tried him with a punning verse, while a cuckoo sang. This is what the verse said:

"The cuckoo above the clouds, how does it mount?" But it meant, "Like the cuckoo to soar so high, how is it so?" To which Yorimasa answered, filling in the necessary couplet, "The waning moon sets not at will," which might also mean, in modest disclaimer of ambitious effort, "Only my bow I bent; that alone sent the shaft." And so this moon stands in the picture, as in the verses, for the bent bow of Yorimasa.

It is a shorter story, that which makes the allusion in the type of the chrysanthemum and the fox. It is a variation of the perpetual story. The prince royal of India had a lovely mistress, who had bewitched him, and who fell asleep one day in a bed of chrysanthemums, where her lover shot at and wounded a fox in the forehead. The bleeding temple of the girl discovered the evil animal she really was. For the fox, as in China, is in Japan a wicked animal, capable of everything in the way of transformation and suggestion.

There are endless stories about him, and the belief or superstition is still very strong. O—— was talking to us lately about the sorcerers and spiritual mediums and fortune-tellers, and, as an explanation of the power of some medium, told us that he claimed to have in his service tame foxes. Only, when I asked where they might be lodged in the little city house, he explained that they were not living in the body, and therefore cumbersome, but were the spirits of foxes, thus subservient, and able to penetrate everywhere and report.

The badger also is a misleading creature, and the cat is considered uncertain.

Or take the way in which Hokusai refers to ancient story when, at the end of one of his books, he makes a picture of the devoted knight Kojima Takanori clad in armor, covered with the peasant's rain-cloak; and he is writing on the trunk of the cherry-tree the message of warning for his master, the Emperor Go-Daigo Tenno. But instead of the old verse, Hokusai has put: "In the sixth year of the era Tempo, in the month of April, my seventy-sixth year, this is written by me, formerly by name Hokusai, but now more correctly known as 'The Old Man gone Mad for Painting.'"

Here I have been wandering into Japan, while my theme was rather the persistence of Chinese subjects, or of subjects connected with China, the list of which would be endless, from Shoki, the devil-killer, hunting his prey of imps over sword-guards and round the corners of boxes, to pictures of aphorisms, such as this saying of Confucius, of which I found a drawing yesterday: "Avoid even the appearance of evil; do not stop to tie your shoes in the melon-patch of an enemy." And so these innumerable subjects are common property, and serve as a field for the artist to try to be himself, to bring out the story or part of it, or his way of looking at it, or its decorative capacity, or any way of anchoring the Japanese imagination. I cannot say that for many of the ordinary arrangements, the most simple and conventional, one does not often suffer the boredom of repetition, as we do at home, with the eagle and the stars, and armorial bearings, and the stereotyped symbolism of churches. But it suffices to see the thing well done again, to start once more into some new enjoyment of the choice of subject.

So there can exist with regard to these subjects, apparently mere motives of form, and partly because they are conventional, a deeper convention or meaning, more or less visible to the artist when at work, according to his temperament or his school, as in our poetry, where an idea may or may not be overlaid with realistic or esthetic decoration.

I reach out for the first design that my hand can find, which turns out to be a drawing by Chin-nan-pin. I have chosen at haphazard, but the choice is perhaps all the better. We shall have no example of a great man to deal with, but merely the work of a remarkable Chinaman who, somewhere in the early eighteenth century, happened to come to Japan, or to be born there, so as to fit into a certain Chinamania then prevalent. The photograph that I send you is a poor one. You can merely discern the pattern, or what might be called the masses, of the design. A horse is tied to a tree,—a horse of Japan,—and a monkey slides down the trunk and clutches at the halter that prevents escape. I need not ask you to admire the stealthy and yet confident step of the ape, and the motions and repugnance and fright of the horse. I don't think that they could be better given. Withal, there is a gravity of general outline and appearances, and a pleasantly managed balance of the full and empty spaces. But these decorative points are not those I wish to refer to just now. What I wish to indicate now is that this subject, which might have suited a Dutch-man for realism and for its choice of the accidental, will mean, if you wish to see it, the natural resistance and struggle of the inferior nature against a superior mastery which it does not understand, and which at first appears capricious and unreasonable. Without being quite certain of the accuracy of my definition, I know that the design is based upon a like convention.

This may not be spirituality, but how far it is from what we call realism, and how wise the acceptance by the artist of a convention which allows him to give all his energies to a new interpretation, through his own study of nature! As with those who have chosen distinctly religious subjects, and whose vitality and personality can triumph and coexist with the absence of novelty in the theme, so the artist in more ordinary subjects may be wise in keeping to themes which are known to those whom he addresses, and in which they can fully grasp and enjoy his success. These general themes allow a stricter individuality in the artist who uses them, when he is capable, and make his want of individuality tolerable, and even laudable and pleasant, when, like most of us, he has little of his own. Then he can never be so offensive if we do not like him. Those that we do not like are often offensive because their personal vanity appears upon a solid ground of their own stupidity. Perhaps this is why the Japanese *objet d'art* never offends, at least in the older work done under the general influences that have obtained with the race.

Hence, also, their astonishing variety. A thousand times, many thousand times, you will have seen the same subject, but never the same rendering, never the same *object*, twice repeated. That is to say, that whenever it is worth while we can get at the most valuable and costly part of the work of art, the humanity that made it, the love of something that went with the work. It is this that makes the mystery of the charm of innumerable little pieces of older work, like the metal-work that belongs to the old swords, any one of which is superior to anything that we do, unless in the rare cases when we bring in the expensive life of a great master to rival it—some part of the work left by a Barye, a Cellini, a Pisano.

All that our great men have done is exactly opposite to the tendency of our modern work, and is based on the same ground that the Japanese has lived and worked on — *i. e.,* the reality and not the appearance, the execution and not the proposition of a theme. The whole principle is involved in the analysis of, say, a successful study from nature — a beautiful painting, for instance, of a beautiful sky. In such a case the subject is all provided; the importance of the result depends upon the artist's sensitiveness to the facts supplied to him, upon his use of his hereditary and acquired methods of recording them, and upon his personal variation of those methods. No one dreams of praising the art of the sky itself, that is to say, the fact that the facts existed; to praise the artist for the thing having occurred from which he worked. It is this apparent want of comprehension of the first principles of the plastic arts in our poor work, and in a vast proportion of our best, that makes any reasonable man a pessimist as to our near future. Every poor element of our civilization is against it, and our influences are now deteriorating the art of Japan. We value material or the body instead of workmanship or the right use of the body; and instead of style and design, the intellect and the heart. To us a gold object seems spiritually precious, and we hesitate at working in other than costly materials. To the Japanese workman wood and gold have been nothing but the means to an end. We had rather not do anything than do anything not enduring, so that when our materials are difficult, the life has flown that was to animate them; the Japanese is willing to build a temporary architecture, and make a temporary lacquer, which holds more beauty and art than we to-day manage to get in granite or in metal.

And when the Oriental workman takes the hardest surfaces of steel or of jade, he has had the preparations for using it with mastery; it is again plastic and yielding for him, as the less abiding materials have been before. Nor would the Japanese artist understand the point of view of many of our men, who do their best to put an end to all art, so lost are they in our vanity of "advertisement." The Japanese would never have invented the idea of doing poorly the work one is forced to do to live, so as to reserve vast energy for more important or influential work that might draw attention to him. The greater part of our "decoration" is carried out just the contrary way to his. Our artists accept as a momentary curse the fact that to live they may have to draw patterns, or work in glass, or paint or model subsidiary ornamentation. They look forward to the glorious time when they may wreak their lofty souls in the dignity of paint mixed with the sacred linseed oil, or in the statue done in bronze or carved in marble by other hands than theirs. And yet if their nature be not too far removed from ours, the habit of doing less than their best, the habit of doing poorly, the scorn of anything but the fine clothes of a fine material, will never be gotten over, and throughout this little cheapness of soul, this essential snobbishness, will be felt to puzzle and disconcert those who wish to admire.

That is to say, that they too often do not look to the end, but to the means, while to the artist the means are a mere path — as with the Greeks, whose work will live, even if its very physical existence is obliterated, because it is built in the mind, in the eternity of thought. So Greek art existed, and has lived, and lives, the most flourishing and richest that we know of — with less to represent it than we turn out daily. So it lived, when it had no longer anything of its own body to represent it, in everything that was done in every country which kept its lessons; and lives still, without examples to refer to, even into the very painting of to-day. It is the principle of the proper place of means that makes the little piece of Japanese metal-work — for instance, the sword-guard or the knife-handle—an epitome of art, certainly a greater work of art than any modern cathedral. And as certainly we shall never even produce good ordinary ornamental work until we feel the truth that I have lamely indicated.

"I might perhaps do as well as this," said an intelligent architect, as we looked at some excellent but not noblest details of French Renaissance, "but how could I spend the time on it? And not only that, but how could I have spent the time previous to this in doing other similar work to train me? I can only make a project, have it carried out by the best commercial firm, not anxious to change the course of trade, and shut my eyes to the result. I should never be criticised, because I did not give more than my bargain." And yet to give more than your bargain is merely to give art.

Look at this little *netsuke*,[1] or *inro*,[2] or sword-guard, and follow the workman as you admire each detail of the execution. He has chosen some subject or some design which may have an associated meaning, or may be of good omen, and bear good wishes, or he may have chosen out of the entire world of observation, of fancy, or of tradition; and may have chosen just as much because it fits well the space which he has to cover.

He will take as well a design that has been used a hundred times as a newer one. For he has to *reinvent* it in execution, even as the Greek sculptor who recut again the "egg and dart," or the orator who is to expound and carry out to success some argument all ready in his mind—as the old architect who rebuilt a glorious Greek temple upon the rules and canons of proportion that others had used before him. But he has to see that this design in his mind—or nearer yet, perhaps on paper—shall fit the spaces of the material and of

[1] Carved button used for suspending the tobacco-pouch to the belt.
[2] A nest of small boxes carried suspended from the belt.

the object which he is to make, so that that it shall be made, as it were, for that place only. He will then go again to nature,—perhaps working directly from it, perhaps only to his memory of sight,—for remember, that in which we call working from nature—we painters—we merely use a shorter strain of memory than when we carry back to our studios the vision that we wish to note. And more than that, the very way in which we draw our lines, and mix our pigments, in the hurry of instant record, in the certainty of successful handling, implies that our mind is filled with innumerable memories of continuous trials.

The workman then goes to nature, and finds in it the reality and the details of his design, even, let us say, to the very markings of a tree trunk that he has chosen; they are all there, since they exist in the design, and the design is good. But they exist only in so far as they exist also in the ivory that he cuts—in the veining of the tortoise-shell or malachite that is to render it. Now with patient pleasure he can hunt out these associations; he can use gold, or silver, or vulgar lead, or lacquer, or the cutting and filing of steel, or the iridescence of mother-of-pearl for his leaves, or his stems, or the water, or the birds—for the clouds or the moonlight,—for the sunshine and the shadow,—for the light and dark,—for the "male and female" of his little manufactured world.

These he will model, chisel, sink, or emboss as the story needs, and do it coarsely, or loosely, or minutely, or delicately, as the unity of his little world requires. And he will work in a hurry, or work slowly, he will varnish it and rub it down, and polish it again, and bake it many times, and let it weather out of doors, or shut it up carefully from the smallest track of dust, or bathe it in acids or salts, and all this for days and months in the year. And when he has finished,—because to do more or less would not be to finish it,—he has given me, besides the excellency of what we call workmanship, which he must give me because that is the bargain between us — he has given me his desires, his memories, his pleasures, his dreams, all the little occurrences of so much life. As you see, he is following the law of *Tao*, so that however humble his little world, it has a life of its own which cannot be separated from its materials; no picture of it, no reproduction, will give its full charm, any more than a photograph gives that of a human being. Take out the word Japanese wherever I have put it, take out the actual materials that I have mentioned, and the description and the reasoning will apply. That is all there is to any work of art. It does not exist in a fine abstract of intention — nor again in the application of some method of toil — to define "technic," as so many young idiots most excusably try to persuade themselves. It exists in an individual result with origins so powerful and deep that they are lost in shade.

To go on, I wish to put it that the same reasons will cause the artist, then, to elaborate profusely, to work in long patience, to use precious materials, to work slightly or carelessly, to finish his work with minute details, or to sketch rapidly with the end of a brush filled with the single color of India ink.

There is no difference in reality; there is only the question of the kind of interest he wishes to evoke, the sort of relation he wishes to establish between himself and his work, and incidentally to me, the looker-on.

I am afraid that this hazy weather is affecting the sequence of my dreaming, or what I am pleased to call my thought, so that you may not clearly understand me.

Again I wish you to remark that in all fullness of work other things are suggested than those directly represented, upon the same principle, for the same reasons, that the successful sketch, as I said before, is richer than it looks. Hence the suggestion of color when there is really but black and white; hence the suggestion of modeled light and shadow when there is really but flat color and outlines. Hence the success of all great periods in what we call decorative work, because there was no separation; there was merely art to be used to fill certain spaces, and to recall the fact that it was so used.

Many years ago I used to read Mr. Ruskin, when "my sight was bad, and I lived within the points of the compass," and also the works of other men, who laid down the exact geography and the due distances, north and south, of a certain department or land of art which they called "Decoration." Some of them are not yet dead. The light of *Tao* fell upon the subject from the words of a child who had been listening to a talk in which I and others wiser than myself were trying to follow out these boundaries that outlined "true" methods of decorative art, and kept to the received instructions of abstention from this and that, of refraining from such and such a reality, of stiffening the flow of outline, of flattening the fullness of modeling, of turning our backs on light and shade, of almost hating the surface of nature; and we wondered that when our European exemplars of to-day had fulfilled every condition of conventionality, had carefully avoided the use of the full methods of art, in the great specialties of painting and sculpture, their glorious work had less stuff to it than a Gothic floral ornament or a Japanese painted fan. "Father," said the child, "are you not all making believe? Is the Japanese richness in their very flat work so different from what you can see in this sketch by my little brother? See how his tree looks as if it had light and shadow, and yet he has used no modeling. He has used only the markings of the tree and their variation of colour to do for both. He has left out nothing, and yet it is flat painting."

Nor have the Japanese *left out* things. They have not been

97

forced to overstudy any part, so as to lose the look of free choice, to make the work assume the appearance of task-work—the work of a workman bored, nobly bored perhaps, but still bored, a feeling that is reflected in the mind of the beholder. The Japanese artist makes his little world,—often nothing but an India-ink world,—but its occupants live within it. They are always obedient to all the laws of nature that they know of.

However piercing the observation of actual fact, its record is always a synthesis. I remember many years ago looking over some Japanese drawings of hawking with two other youngsters, one of them now a celebrated artist, the other a well-known teacher of science. What struck us then was the freedom of record, the acute vision of facts, the motions and actions of the birds, their flight, their attention, and their resting, the alertness and anxiety of their hunters, and the suggestions of the entire landscapes (made with a few brush-marks). One saw the heat, and the damp, and the dark meandering of water in the swamps; marked the dry paths which led over sounding wooden bridges, and the tangle of weeds and brush, and the stiff swaying of high trees. All was to us realism, but affected by an unknown charm.

Now this is what the artist who did this realism has said, as well as I can make it out: "The ancient mode must be maintained. Though a picture must be made like the natural growth of all things, yet it lacks taste and feeling if it simulates the real things."

Evidently the painter had not learned our modern distinctions of the realist and the idealist.

If you wished to know what I admire most in these forms of art, I might say to you, keeping, I hope, within the drift of what I have been writing, that it is their obedience to early rules which were once based on the first primeval needs of the artist. And if you pushed me further, and wished to make me confess what I thought that these necessities might be, and to make me give you a definition of them, and thereby force me into a definition of art itself, I should hesitatingly state that I do not like to define in matters so far down as causes. But if you would not tell, or take advantage of my having been drawn into such a position of doctrine, I might acknowledge that I have far within me a belief that art is the love of certain balanced proportions and relations which the mind likes to discover and to bring out in what it deals with, be it thought, or the actions of men, or the influences of nature, or the material things in which necessity makes it to work. I should then expand this idea until it stretched from the patterns of earliest pottery to the harmony of the lines of Homer. Then I should say that in our plastic arts the relations of lines and spaces are, in my belief, the first and earliest desires. And again I should have to say that, in my un-expressed faith, these needs are as needs of the soul, and echoes of the laws of the universe, seen and unseen, reflections of the universal mathematics, cadences of the ancient music of the spheres.

For I am forced to believe that there are laws for our eyes as well as for our ears, and that when, if ever, these shall have been deciphered, as has been the good fortune with music, then shall we find that all best artists have carefully preserved their instinctive obedience to these, and have all cared to-gether for this before all.

For the arrangements of line and balances of spaces which meet these underlying needs are indeed the points through which we recognize the answer to our natural love and sen-sitiveness for order, and through this answer we feel, clearly or obscurely, the difference between what we call great men and what we call the average, whatever the personal charm may be.

This is why we remember so easily the arrangement and composition of such a one whom we call a master—that is why the "silhouette" of a Millet against the sky, why his placing of outlines within the rectangle of his picture, makes a different, a final, and decisive result, impressed strongly upon the memory which classifies it, when you compare it with the record of the same story, say, by Jules Breton. It is not the difference of the fact in nature, it is not that the latter artist is not in love with his subject, that he has not a poetic nature, that he is not simple, that he has not dignity, that he is not exquisite; it is that he has not found in nature of his own instinct the eternal mathematics which accompany facts of sight. For indeed, to use other words, in what does one differ from the other? The arrangement of the idea or subject may be the same, the costume, the landscape, the time of day, nay, the very person represented. But the Millet, if we take this instance, is framed within a larger line, its spaces are of greater or more subtle ponderation, its building together more architectural. That is to say, all its spaces are more surely related to *one another*, and not only to the *story told*, nor only to the *accidental occurrence* of the same. The eternal has been brought in to sustain the transient.

For fashions change as to feelings and sentiments and ways of looking at the world. The tasks of the days of Angelico, or of Rubens, or of Millet are not the same; religions live and disappear; nations come and go in and out of the pages of history: but I can see nothing from the earliest art that does not mean living in a like desire for law and order in expression. It is, therefore, because we consciously or unconsciously recognize this love of the unwritten harmonies of our arts, the power of recalling them to us, in some painter or in some architect, that we say that such a man is great. He is great because he is the same as man has been, and will be; and we recognize, without knowing them by name, our ancestral primordial predilections.

Yes, the mere direction or distance of a line by the variation of some fraction of an inch establishes this enormous superiority—a little more curve or less, a mere black or white or colored space of a certain proportion, a few darks or reds or blues. And now you will ask, Do you intend to state that decoration—? To which I should say, I do not mean to leave my main path of principles to-day, and when I return we shall have time to discuss objections. Besides, "I am not arguing; I am telling you."

This is the unity, this is the reality, which disengages itself from the art of Japan, even as we know it in common, through what we usually call "bric-à-brac." Our introduction to it is rather curious when one comes to think of it. Suddenly, owing to enormous social changes in Japan, involving vast fluctuations in fortunes, most of all that was portable was for sale, and flooded our markets. Ignorant dealers held in masses small treasures of temples, adornments of the wealthy, all the odds and ends of real art, along with the usual furniture, along with all the poor stuff that would naturally be made for us barbarians, and had been made for us for centuries through the trade of Holland. It was as if Paris or London had suddenly been unloaded of everything portable, from works of art to household furniture. Naturally the mainspring of it all,—the works of great draftsmen, for instance,—being more debatable, more inexplicable, more useless, in a word, or detained by stronger bands, just as it would be with us, have somewhat escaped the drain. Our perceptions have been confused in all this mixture by repetitions, imitations, which in every form of art, as we know so well in literature, degrade the perception and enjoyment of what is good. I can only wonder that the world has not been tired out and disgusted with Japanese bric-à-brac. And had we not been in such bad straits of taste ourselves, such would have been the case. I have always considered that the artist needed to be forgiven for his turn toward bric-à-brac; not for his liking to have odds and ends for help and refreshment, but for having too many; because his life is to make, not to collect. To others, that can be forgiven easily; for the pieces of the past are a consolation of the present, and one would like to feel that a man's likings are his important self, and are betrayed by his choices. "Dis-moi ce que tu aimes—je te dirai ce que tu es."

If one had time and did not do, what pleasure it might be to describe forever the innumerable objects and things that might be found here, even though words are a poor rendering of sight. And what pleasure it might be to try to describe the greatest of all bric-à-brac, the greatest remains of the higher arts—sculpture and painting.

I have begun some such letter for you, but I fear that it may never be finished. Nor do I see any way of giving an account of the history of painting in Japan, which would have to stand for a still further explanation. Should I study it further, can I do more than to increase my own know-ledge,—and all knowledge is a burden,—and to give you cursory proof, by names and a few examples, that the art of painting and the art of sculpture are very old here? I should have to begin to ask myself for you if the earliest remains do not already prove still earlier schools and accepted or debated tradition, and I should then have still one thousand years of design to account for.

I shall probably leave my letter to you unfinished. It has already become unwieldy, and I could give you only my own impressions. And then in the history of art everything is needed.

It would not be merely reproduction in words, however beautiful, of the surfaces of works that have survived time, nor of the men who made them, of their characters, the accidents of their lives, and their technical beliefs. It would be simply a history of humanity at a given place. It could not be solved by a mere account of the place and the race, according to some of our later scientific fads. I was writing to you but yesterday, and trying to make out that the work of art is often a contradiction of the period, or a step in advance; that the moods of feeling of the future are as often reflected by art as the habits of the present. But whatever personal sense of solitariness or of antagonism has inspired or oppressed the artist, he must have had partners since he has had admirers, even when he antagonizes his time. However transient certain of his forms, however much to us who come afterward they indicate the *period*, he has expressed not his time, but the needs of others who have been looking in the same ways, and yet have had no voice. And even if they have not quite sympathized, the accumulations of like tendencies have become stronger and clearer in their descendants. To reflect fully, then, in words, the face of the work of art, one would have to melt into it in some way the gaze of those who have looked at it; to keep upon it still the gentle looks of the pitiful and the loving, the rapt contemplation of the saints, the tender or mocking smile of women, the hard or contemptuous appreciation of rulers, the toleration of the wise, all of which have been in reality a part of the very work. Their negations or sympathies have fallen on the work, and these ineffable delicacies of impression are transmitted in it to successive generations, even as the shadowing of innumerable years of incense-burning has browned the gold and blackened the azure, as concealment in the shade has sometimes paled, sometimes preserved, the edges of the outlines and the modeling of the colors, or exposure and heat and damp have cracked and channeled and dusted all surfaces. You see what I should consider a true carrying out of such a task, and how unsatisfied I should be with anything that I could accomplish, unless it were to stand to you as something fragmentary and evanescent. One thing I should like to do,—should I remain long enough, and be able to get it from the few acquaintances who may know,—and that is, to save some part of the artists themselves out of that obscurity by which the lives of great workers are almost always clouded. To me Rembrandt, and Balzac, and Delacroix, each contradictory to his surroundings, have become more intelligible through the record of their every-day struggle, the exactness of measurement which one can place upon the personal circumstances in which they carried out their work, the limitations of its exact meaning and importance in their own eyes, as we follow them in the daylight of favor, or in the gloomy endings that so often close the lives of great artists.

I hear occasionally of the wanderings of Kano Motonobu, the founder of the great school and family of artists who have lasted through four centuries to the present day, and have filled Japan and the temples here with works better or poorer, until the family name becomes a burden. I hear about Okio, the charmer, the painter of everything and of animals, who began as a little child, by sketching on the earth with bamboo sticks when he followed his parents into the fields to work. One might perhaps learn about Hokusai, who is tabooed here, and about whom I dare not inquire, but whose charming last letter, as given by Mr. Morse, comes back to my memory—it is so gay and so sad, so triumphant over circumstances, so expressive of the view of the world which explains his woodcuts. I quote from memory: "King Em-mā" (he writes to a friend)—"King Em-mā" (the ruler of the under world) "has become very old, and is thinking of retiring from business; so that he has ordered a little country house to be built, and he asks of me to come to him that I may paint him a 'kakemono'; so that in a few days I must be ready to travel and to take my sketches with me. I shall take up my residence at the corner of the Street of the Under World, where it will give me much pleasure to receive thee, when thou hast the opportunity to come over there."

Or this mocking challenge to old age, at the end of one of the volumes of his pictures of Fuji:

"Since my sixth year I have felt the impulse to represent the form of things; by the age of fifty I had published numberless drawings; but I am displeased with all I have produced before the age of seventy. It is at seventy-three that I have begun to understand the form and the true nature of birds, of fishes, of plants, and so forth. Consequently, by the time I get to eighty, I shall have made much progress; at ninety, I shall get to the essence of things; at a hundred, I shall have most certainly come to a superior, undefinable position; and at the age of a hundred and ten, every point, every line, shall be alive. And I leave it to those who shall live as I have myself, to see if I have not kept my word. Written, at the age of seventy-five, by me, formerly known as Hokusai, but now known as Gakyo Rojin (The Old Man gone Mad for Painting)."

. . . I had been intending to add, when I interrupted myself some way back, that I enjoyed in this art of Japan—at least in this drawing which they call painting—the strange nearness I seem to be in to the feelings of the men who did the work. There is between us only a thin veil of consummate skill. The habit and the methods resulting from it, of an old obedience to an unwritten law common to all art, have asked for the directest ways of marking an intention or an observation.

This reference to a previous tradition of meaning, of ideal arrangement by rule, this wish for synopsis, this feeling for manners of expressing one's self in the thing seen, will naturally make art out of anything. And it is not wonderful that what we call handwriting may then give full play to art, in a written language of which ideography is the key. Given the Chinese characters, their original intentions, the associations, historical and literary, connected with them, is it anything strange in reality, however strange to our habits, to find writing a form of art in Japan? It may have all I have just referred to, and be full of the meaning of ideas, and be literature, and then it can be made conformable to the laws of beauty of form and spacing; and above all, to give character of style, and character of personality, to look more or less grave, or elegant, or weighty, according to circumstances, be elegiac, or lyric, or epic, and reflect on its face the intentions of the text. And again it will be the mark or *sign* of the person; so that my Japanese friends can object to Hokusai's bad writing, as betraying something not refined, for a weighty argument against his other works done with a similar implement, the brush, which is the pen of the far East.

It will then be in what we call drawing—which is an abstraction, the synopsis of the outlines of things meeting together, of their relative intensities, of their own colors, of their relations to the place they are in, that is to say, the picture—that this art of Japan, the daughter of the art of China, will attain its highest form; so that in reality those of us who think of it as appearing at its best only in color, in external charm, have not understood it. An etching of Rembrandt could fairly be said to represent, not so much in itself, but in its essence, what a great Chinaman would have liked to do in India ink—the material of all others which, even to us, is his especially. The line, the abstract line of Rembrandt, its elegance, its beautiful patterning of the surface, is concealed to us by the extraordinary richness of some of his modeling and the extreme gradations of what we call light and shade. But it is there all the same, as a geologic foundation, in the same way that inside of the Titian's splendor of surface there is a decorative substructure as well balanced and fixed as a Venetian brocade—just as the works of other great colorists, as we call them (to designate more complex men), imply, in their constitution and the mechanism of their technic, powers of design and drawing sufficient to furnish out armies of such draftsmen as flourish, for instance, in the Paris of to-day. It is this surplus of richness that conceals the identity. Our arts have undertaken an enormous accession of truths and ambitions upon which the arts of the extreme East have never ventured. They have attained their end, the end of all art, at an earlier mental period. They are younger, perhaps even more like children, and their work cannot involve the greater complications of greater age; but it has also all that grasp of the future that belongs to youth, and that has to be accompanied by deficiences of knowledge; that is to say, of later acquirement and the practice of good and evil. And it is impossible to, look at the expression of nature, or of any intention made by the child in full sincerity, without realizing that the aim of the artist, be he even Michael Angelo, is to return to a similar directness and unity of rendering. Not that the Eastern artist, any more than the child, could be conscious of deficiencies of which he had not thought. He has been satisfied, as we have been satisfied, but for a longer time and under a greater prestige. As the fruit painted by the Greek deceived the birds, and the curtain painted by the Greek painter deceived his fellow-artist, so the horses of Kanaoka have escaped from their "kakemonos," and the tigers sculptured in the lattices of temples have been known to descend at night and rend one another in the courtyards. O—— tells me the Chinese story of the painter forced to let go his painting of the moon for a nominal sum to repay an oppressive moneylender, and how, when the banker happened to unroll it, the whole room was illumined, and he grew into a habit of spending evenings in the mild effulgence

107

of the painted rays. But when, after an absence, he looked at it again, the moon was gone,—where old moons go,—and he was enraged at the painter, though he might well have noticed that for many days the moon had not been so bright, and indeed had seemed to be ill drawn. O—— tells me that the artist got it back for little, and waited the necessary number of days to have its crescent reappear again; and A—— says that, though the picture is lost to-day, he hopes to find it again in China in following years.

These stories serve as a way of stating to you that as long as new wants were not felt, newer accuracies did not begin to exist, and these limitations are naturally seen to be more easily put up with in a civilization of uninterrupted tradition. To acquire something when one's hands are full, something has to be dropped. In the stations of our own progress in art, the advance has at every stage involved some deficiency, or failure, or weakening on another side. This is the only explanation I can make for painting in the extreme East not having taken up portraiture—that is to say, not having triumphed in it, while sculpture has reached out toward it in a splendid way. We have seen the same thing in the transition from the Middle Ages, when sculpture outreaches painting in the direction of reality. But then sculpture is to a certain extent easier and in a certain way inferior, because it gives a sort of duplicate of the object, not a relation of it to other things.

So that the Japanese have not come to the work from the "model," which has at so many periods and so long been ours. Theirs are types of types; they are not, as with us, persons, and the pursuit of beauty in the individual has not been followed apparently by the art of the far East. The personal love and preference of the artist embodied in another person their art does not show; nor have their artists given a nameless immortality to certain human beings, so that for ages their types, their images, their moods, their characters, their most transitory variations of beauty, have been proposed to us as an example. Have you ever reflected how the nameless model reigns in the memory of man with a personal fame more intimate than that of Cheops, or Helen, or Cæsar, because the artist has been obliged to build upon this person his own dream of the world—as with the Roman girl who is the Madonna of San Sisto?

   .   .   .   So, again, the Eastern artists have suggested, and implied, and used light and shade, and perspective, and anatomy, and the relations of light to color, and of color to light, only so much as they could take into their previous scheme.

In many cases their success is still an astonishment to us. Certainly their records of motion, their construction of plants and flowers and birds, we have all appreciated; and their scientific, easy noting of colored light in landscape made even Rousseau dream of absorbing its teaching into his pictures, which certainly represent the full Western contradictory idea, in the most complicated acceptance of every difficulty.

The artist here, then, has not made separate analytical studies of all the points that trouble us, that have cost at times some acquirement of the past, in the anxiety for working out a new direction; as to-day, for instance, in learned France, where the very art of painting, as a mirror of the full-colored appearance of things, has for a quarter of a century been in peril, under the influence of the academy drawing-school, the model in studio light, and the vain attempt to rival the photograph. And perhaps it is needless to repeat again how we have lost the sense of natural decoration and expression of meaning by general arrangement of lines and spaces, so that again in France we are astonished at M. Puvis de Chavannes, who uses powers that have once been common to almost all our race.

Here the artist does not walk attired in all the heavy armor which we have gradually accumulated upon us. His learning in side issues is not unnecessarily obtruded upon me, so as to conceal the sensitiveness of his impressions or the refinement of his mind. As for us, we have marched on in a track parallel to science, striving now for centuries to subdue the material world—to get it into the microcosm of our paintings. Each successive great generation has taken up the task, heavier and heavier as time goes on, halting and resting when some new "find" has been made, working out a new discovery often with the risk of the loss of a greater one.

But how often the processes have covered up what is most important,—to me at least,—the value of the individual, his aspirations, and indeed the notions or beliefs that are common between us.

Sometimes this covering has been sordid and mean, pedantic or unesthetic, sometimes most splendid. But how difficult it has been always for the many to read, for instance, in our great Rubens, the evidences of a lofty nature, the devout intentions of a healthy mind!

Not that we can turn back to-day and desert. From the time when the Greek first asserted in art the value of personal manhood to the date of the "impressionist" of to-day, the career has been one. And certainly in the art of painting a vaster future lies before us, whenever we are ready to carry the past. But remember that whatever has been really great once will always remain great.

Even if I were competent to make more than approaches to reflection, this place of dreams is not well chosen for effort. I feel rather as if, tired, I wished to take off my modern armor, and lie at rest, and look at these pictures of the simplicity of attitude in which we were once children. For, indeed, the meaning of our struggle is to regain that time, through toil and the fullness of learning, and to live again in the oneness of mind and feeling which is to open to us the doors of the kingdom.

SKETCHING

NIKKO SAN, August 12.

THE enchantment of idleness is no longer to be lived in, of mere enjoyment of what I see. I have now to feel the bitterness of work, of effort of memory and analysis, and to become responsible to myself for what I see, and for the accuracy with which I see it; just as my quieting inhalation of the Buddhist air is disturbed by the intellectual necessity of giving to myself some account of formulas, and later, unfortunately, of rendering to you this same account of my impressions. And yet I feel so delightfully lazy, so much as if I were in a Newport in which all should be new. All this place has become more and more enchanting. I am sure that I shall go with the regret of not having painted whatever I shall leave untried; all so preferable, undoubtedly, to what shall have been done. Everything here exists for a painter's delight, everything composes or makes pleasant arrangements, and the little odds and ends are charming, so that I sometimes feel as if I liked the small things that I have discovered better than the greater which I am forced to recognize.

And, then, all looks wild and natural, as if undisturbed by man; but no one can tell in a place where nature is so admirable, so admired, and so adored.

I like the old roads between *yashiki* walls, broken up with torrents and bridges; and the small shrines and sacred trees, which have no great point but that they are pretty, and so far away—in the infancy of the world. Stones and rocks that are sacred—why and wherefore no one exactly knowing; only that it is so, and has been so for a long, long time.

Three thousand years ago Europe was so, with paganism—the peasant or earth belief—gradually lost to our comprehension except through hearsay. So we are accustomed to write of the sacred grove; and here it is, all about me, as if history were made living. The lovely scenery reminds me continually of what has been associated with it; a civilization which has been born of it, has never separated from nature, has its religion, its art, and its historic associations entangled with all natural manifestations. The great Pan might still be living here, in a state of the world which has sanctified trees and groves, and associated the spirit-world with every form of the earthly dwelling-place. I feel as if I were nearer than I can be through books to the old world we try to rebuild by collation of facts and documents.

Could a Greek come back here he would find his "soul-informed rocks," and all that he thought divine or superstitious, even to the very "impressions of Aphrodite." The sacredness that lives here in mountains would seem all natural to him, as would the stories of mountain gods who ages ago met here the advance of the Buddhist priests. For Buddhism has joined with the earthly faith in attaching religious value to solitary places and mountain heights, and many are the stories which link these two beliefs from the early times. As, for instance, when Shodo Shonin in his wanderings came here and "opened up" the mountains of Nikko. For this saintly discoverer, dwelling in early youth among sacred caves, and a devout reverer of the native and Buddhist deities, had long dreamed of wondrous things on distant mountains, of celestial or spiritual beings, visible even to the eye, and pursued his search according to holy vows and under celestial guidance.

Where the red lacquer bridge now goes over the Dayagawa,

Shodo Shonin first crossed upon the fairy snake bridge, which, like a rainbow spanning the hills, was thrown over for him by a mysterious colossal god of the mountain. Here, a few yards off, he built the shrine in honor of his helper, the "great King of the Deep Sand." This was in the year 767 of our era; and in 782, after much previous exploration, he reached the summit of Nan-tai-san, and met the tutelary gods of Nikko, who promised to watch over the welfare of Japan and the progress of the new religion. These three gods were long worshiped thereafter at the foot of the mountain, on the bank of the lake named Chiuzenji, by him, along with the Buddhist incarnations whose temple he established there. So that these primordial divinities were looked upon by certain Buddhist eyes as what they named "temporary manifestations" of the great essences known as Amida, Buddha, and Kuwan-on.

Last evening, near the back of the rock upon which is the tomb of Iyéyasŭ, I followed some zigzag stone steps that lead up to a little shrine, dark among the trees, in which is the figure of an old man with powerful legs—the master pilgrim Enno-Sho-kaku. Why his shrine was exactly there I have not clearly made out; but certainly, as a mountain spirit, his being here is appropriate. For, born a miraculous child, he loved from infancy the solitariness of woods far up the mountains. The rain never wet him; no living things of the forest were ever hurt by him, even through chance; he lived, as they might, on nuts and berries, clothed in the tree's own dress, of the tendrils of the wistaria. Thus he passed forty years among mountains and waterfalls, under directions received in dreams, to bring the wild places beneath the dominion of Buddha. Two hill spirits served him and provided him with fuel and water. The life of nature became his, and he moved through water or through air as easily as his mind dwelt in the present and in the future.

Naturally, too, when he touched the world of men he was

maligned and persecuted; but even then, when exiled to an island in the sea, he could fly back at night to revisit his mother, or ascend his beloved mountains, while submitting obediently in the daylight to the presence of his guards. Naturally, too, his evil days came to an end, and he was freed, and finally flitted away toward China, and has never reappeared. With him in the little shrine are his faithful imps, painted red and green, and out of the darkness his wooden image, with a long white beard, looked absolutely real in the rainy twilight. Enormous iron sandals hung on every side, offerings of pilgrims anxious to obtain legs as sturdy as those of the pilgrim patron. Had I been able to leave my own I should have done so, for never have I felt as weakened and unenergetic as I have become in this idle climate. We could just see the white stone steps of the little road as we came down the steep hill through the wood to the gate of Iyémitsŭ's tomb.

August 16.

The languor that oppresses me does not disappear, and I live with alternations of exertion that reflect the weather. There has been an immense amount of sunshine and the same amount of rain, compressing into a single day as much as would suffice at home for weeks of summer and winter. Suddenly, from hot blue skies, come down the cloud and the wet. The lovely little hills or mountains opposite our house round out, all modeled and full, in a glossy green, to be painted in another hour with thin washes of gray, thickened with white, as in the single-colored designs of the old Limoges enamels. Then their edges grow sharp and thin, and are stamped against further mists, like pale prints of the Japanese designs, making me see those pictures increased to life-size. And I realize how accurate these are, even to the enlarged appearance of the great trees which fringe their tops and edges, as these are seen through the broken, wet veil of moisture. And even here, again, I am puzzled as to whether art has helped nature.

August 17.

Yesterday I suffered seriously from the heat. I had gone to the little flat table-land that lies to the north behind our house, through which runs a small road, untraveled and grass-grown, connecting somewhere or other with the road of the great temples. I had intended to study there, for several reasons; one, among others, because I saw every day, as I looked through my screens, a little typical landscape-picture of Japan. Near by, a small temple shrine all vermilion in the sun, with heavy, black, oppressive roof; then a stretch of flat table-land, overgrown with trees and bushes, from which stood up a single high tree, with peaceful horizontal branches; on each side, conical hills, as if the wings of a stage-scene; far beyond, a tumble of mountains behind the great depression of the river hidden out of sight; and above, and farther yet, the great green slopes that lead to the peak of Nio-ho. It was very hot, and all the clouds seemed far away, the sun very high in the early noon, and no shade. I passed the new priests' houses of the old temple near us, where are billeted, to the inconvenience of the owners, many sailor boys sent all the way from the navy yard of Okotsuka, so that they escape the cholera, as we are doing. They are usually washing their clothes in the torrent that runs under the bridge of three carved stones, which I have to get into the little path, fre-quented by gadflies, that takes me up to my sketching-ground. Were it not for the amiably obtrusive curiosity of these youngsters in their leisure hours, I should pass through their courtyard into the shady spaces near the little temples and the three-storied pagoda, which the priests' houses adjoin.

116

I am always courteously saluted by the priests, and one of them, living there in vacation, I know. He is off duty at the temples of Iyémitsŭ, and I have seen him at the home of our friends. I send you a sketch of his face, which appears to me impressed by sincerity and a certain anxiety very sympathetic. When I sketch near the pagoda I see him occasionally ringing the hanging-bell or cymbal, with the same step and air of half-unconscious performance of habitual duty that I remember so well in Catholic priests whom I knew as a boy.

Here the memory of Shodo Shonin comes up again, with a confusion of intention in the assembled worship of Buddhist and native divinities. For the "opener of mountains" built the temple here to the same god, with the never-ending name, whom he met on the summit of Nan-tai-san. And the adjoining chapel, dedicated to Kuwanon, means that she was in reality the essential being, behind the temporary manifestation, that assumed the name and appearance of his mountain god, — the *genius loci*. And the Latin words bring back the recollection of curious stones in the mossy green shade, to which is attached the meaning of the oldest past; for they are "male" and "female" — emblems and images of earliest worship, empowered to remind, and perhaps obscurely to influence.

Seated at last under my umbrella, I could feel the hot moisture rising from the grass beneath me. The heated hills on each side wore a thin interlacing of violet in the green of their pines. The mountains across the river were frosted in the sunlight, with the thinnest veil of a glitter of wet.

Between them great walls of vapor rose from the hidden river, twisting into draperies that slowly crawled up the slopes of the great mountain. Far off, its top was capped with cloud, whose mass descended in a shower over its face and between its peaks, and kept all its nearer side in a trembling violet shadow.

Above the peak the great mass of fog spread to the farthest mountains, letting their highest tops shine through with a pale-blue faintness like that of sky. But the great back of the long slope was distinct, and of a vivid green against the background of violet mountains. So solid and close-packed it looked under the high light that one might forget that this green was not of turf, firm under foot, but was a trackless waste of tall grasses high as a man's head. Farther on against the northern sky the eastern slope was golden and sharp. In the highest sky of fiery blue large cumulus clouds shone above and through the fog, whose ragged edge blew like a great flag toward the south. The little temple blazed in vermilion, one side all lighted up, its black-tiled roof hot in the sun. In the shadow of its porch the columns and entablature were white and pale gold and green.

My attempt to render the light and heat lasted for two or three hours: my damp umbrella seemed penetrated by the light, my skin was scorched and blistered, and a faint dizziness kept warning me to get back to a larger shade. When I yielded, I was only just able to reach my welcome mats, saved from something worse by my very scorching. Since yesterday I have been ill; not sleeping, but dreaming uncomfortably; and visited and comforted, however, by our fair hostess and the Doctor.

Murmurs of Buddhistic conversation remain in my mind: vague stories of life in Southern monasteries, of refined ascetic life, of sublimated delicate food, of gentle miraculous powers, known to the favored few that behold them at times; of ascensions and disappearances like those of the pilgrim saint of whom I was telling you yesterday—all of which talk mingles with the vague intent of my painting. For I had proposed to make my studies serve for the picture of the "Ascension"; to use the clouds and the wilderness for my

118

background; and to be, at least for moments, in some relation to what I have to represent; that is to say, in an atmosphere not inimical, as ours is, to what we call the miraculous. Here, at least, I am not forced to consider external nature as separate and opposed, and I can fall into moods of thought,—or, if you prefer, of feeling,—in which the edges of all things blend, and man and the outside world pass into each other.

August 17.

And so, often, I like to think of these trees and rocks and streams, as if from them might be evolved some spiritual essence. Has not Çakyamuni said that all (living) beings possess the nature of Buddha, that is to say, the absolute nature. The sun, the moon, the earth, and the innumerable stars contain within themselves the absolute nature. So for the little flowers, the grass, the clouds that rise from the waters, the very drop of water itself; for they are begotten of nature absolute, and all form a part of it, however great, however small. Absolute nature is the essence of all things, and is the same as all things. This absolute nature will be as are the waters of the sea, if we picture it, and its modes will be as the waves, inseparable from the waters. Thus the absolute and all things will be identical, inseparable views of the same existence. This nature will be both essence and force, and appearance and manner. And so my friends here, of the sect which holds the temple, might teach me that the little plants, the great mountains, and the rushing waters can become Buddhas.

In these pantheistic sympathies I dimly recall that another sect finds three great mysteries in its esoteric view of the world. The wind whistling through the trees, the river breaking over its rocks, the movements of man and his voice,—or, indeed, his silence,—are the expression of the great mysteries of body, of word, and of thought. These

mysteries are understood of the Buddha, but evolution, cultivated by the "true word," or doctrine, will allow man, whose
mysteries are like the mysteries of the Buddhas, to become
like unto them.

But since the path is open for all to Buddhahood, — since
these animals that pass me, this landscape about me, can
become divine, — why, alas! are not men more easily carried
to that glorious end? It is because we are living in the present;
and as that present must have had a past, since nothing is lost
and nothing disappears, so it will have a future; and that
future depends on the present and on the past. Changes and
transformations are only a "play" of cause and effect, since
spirit and matter are one in absolute nature, which in its
essence can neither be born nor be dissolved. Actual life is
absolutely determined by the influencing action of merit and
demerit in past existence, as the future will be determined by
present causes; so that it is possible for the soul to pass
through the six conditions of the infernal being, the phantom,
the beast, the demon, the human, and the celestial, and,
through painful transmigration, to reach the supreme salvation of Nirvana. Then will end the universal metamor-
phoses, the trials, the expiations, the unceasing whirlwind of
life. Illusion will cease, and reality last, in the complete calm
of absolute truth.

NIRVANA

HAVE I told you my story of the word Nirvana, as used by the reporter at Omaha, who managed to interview us? The association of a reporter with any of the four states of Nirvana may seem impossible to you—but this is the way it happened.

Owing to A——'s being the brother of the president of the road, we were naturally suspected of business designs when we acknowledged that we were going to Japan, and, in my shortsighted wisdom, I thought that I should put to rout our interviewer by "allowing" that the purpose of our going was to find Nirvana. I had misjudged the mind of the true reporter, and did not expect the retort, "Are you not rather late in the season?" Whether he knew or "builded better," he had certainly pointed out the probable result. I often recur to this episode when, as now, I enjoy, in dreaming action, that Nirvana which is called conditioned; that state of the terrestrial being who understands truth by the extinction of passions, but who is yet, indeed, very much tied to the body—if I may speak so lightly of what is a contemplation of, and an absorption in, eternal truth, a rest in supreme salvation.

Of all the images that I see so often, the one that touches me most—partly, perhaps, because of the Eternal Feminine—is that of the incarnation that is called Kuwanon, when shown absorbed in the meditations of Nirvana.

You have seen her in pictures, seated near some waterfall,

and I am continually reminded of her by the beautiful scenes about us, of which the waterfall is the note and the charm. Were it not that I hate sightseeing, I should have made pilgrimages, like the good Japanese, to all the celebrated ones which are about. Exercise, however, during the day is difficult to me, and I don't like being carried, and the miserable horses of the peasants are awfully slow and very stumbly. We go about in single file, perched on the saddles upon their humped backs, each horse led by the owner, usually a trousered peasant girl. Lately on our visits to waterfalls we have passed the wide bed of the second river, which makes an island of our mountain — a great mountain-river bed filled with stones and boulders, through which the waters, now very low, divide into rushing torrents; while in the winter this is a tremendous affair, and in flood-times the very boulders are carried away. Far down at Imaichi, some six miles off, is shown one of the long row of stone Buddhas, several hundred in number, which line the right bank of the main river, the Dayagawa, near the deep pool called Kamman-ga-fuchi.

It was there that I drew the biggest of them all, on one of my first days here, a statue of Jizo, with Nan-tai-san half veiled in the distance behind him — a great cedar shading him, and all but the little path and the bridge of a single stone overgrown with weeds and bushes. These gods along the river are all ugly and barbarous, — country gods, as it were, — alien as possible, while the nature about them, though strange, is not so far away from me.

Their ugliness was accentuated by a sort of efflorescence, or moss growth, curled and ragged by weather, made of innumerable slips of paper pasted upon them by troops of pilgrims to the holy places, who make a point of thus marking off their visits to each successive sacred object. Fortunately, they are what the Japanese call "wet goods," that is to say, unprotected by roof or temple, and the rains of heaven cleanse them and leave only the black and white of the lichens. They always worried me like a bad dream when I passed them in the evening, on my way home from work, and I can sympathize with the superstition which makes it impossible to count them. But this is on the Dayagawa, the main confluent which rushes down from Lake Chiuzenji. Our path led through the other river, over causeways and bridges, up to the hills on the other side, and to a high moorland from which the immense southern plain and distant mountains appeared swimming in light. Two faint blue triangles in the air were the peaks of Tsŭkŭba; nearer on the west, the mountains of Nikko were covered with cloud, through which the sunburst poured down upon their bases.

As we rode we passed beneath plantations covered with water, so that their mirror, at the level of the eye, reflected the mountains and clouds and upper sky in a transparent picture, spotted with innumerable tufts of brilliant green. And then we dismounted at a little teahouse, and sat under a rustic arbor, while our feminine grooms, stripping to the waist, wiped and sponged their sweating arm-pits and bosoms, in unconcernedness of sex. Yet when they noticed my sketching them, as if I did not take their nakedness for granted, sleeves and gowns were rapidly pulled over the uncovered flesh. So true it is that conduct depends upon the kind of attention it calls for. Nor was the universal standard of feminine propriety unrespected by them, when, on our return, my guide, who had, in every possible way that I could imagine, expressed her adherence to the ways of nature, met with the disaster of having her back hair come down; for then, with a shriek, she dropped the rein, and retired, blushing, behind the nearest tree, where, in equal hurry, another girl guide proceeded to console her, and to rearrange the proper structure of shining black hair and ivory pins.

Then we descended by a narrow path, over which hung tree-camellias, still spotted with their last white blossoms, whose edges were rusted by the heat.

The main fall of Urami-no-Taki drops into a deep basin, edged by rocks, from a hollow in the highest hill, over which hang great trees. On each side lesser cascades rush or tumble over the rocky faces, and under the main column small streams slide down, or drop in thin pillars to join it. There is a path, frequented by pilgrims, which passes behind and underneath the fall, so that we can stand behind and look through it, whence its name. All is wilderness; but a high relief of the protector Fudo, guardian and friend of such places, is carved on the rock behind the falls, and shows through the rumpled edges of the water. All was shade, except where the sun struck in the emerald hollow above the fall, or where a beam lighted up here and there a patch of the great and small cascades, or the trees and rocks about them. And here, again, the intense silence, broken by the rush of the waterfall, recalled the pictures of K'wan-on, whose meaning and whose images bring back to me the Buddhistic idea of compassion. The deity, or goddess, seated in abstraction by the falling waters of life, represents, I suppose, more especially an ideal of contemplation, as the original Indian name indicated, I think; but her name to-day is that of the Compassionate One.

Of the divinity's many incarnations one has interested me as typical, and will amuse you. It is when—in the year 696 B. C., though the precise date is not exactly material—this power is born as a girl, daughter to one of the many kings of China. Then follows a legend like that of Saint Barbara. She is in no hurry to follow her princess's duty of getting married, and pleasing her parents thereby. She is satisfied with a virgin life, and makes delays by persuading her father to build palaces for her bridal to come; and when all this has been done, and there is no final escape, she ends by an absolute refusal of marriage. At which, evidently from a long experience of the uselessness of argument with her sex, her father cuts her head off, and I regret to say that she thereupon goes to Hell. I suppose that she goes there, because, however laudable and high her ideal of life might have been, it should have been confined within the views of her country, that is to say, of obedience to parents first and foremost. However, she went there, and put up with it, and that so admirably that the divinity who rules the place was obliged to dismiss her, for her contentment with her lot was spreading as an example to the damned, and threatened the very existence of Hell. Since then her appearances again in this world have been on errands of compassion and of help. Nor is this constant willingness to act on behalf of others, and thereby to leave the realm of absolute peace, incompatible with that continual contemplation of which her pictures or images offer an ideal, enchanting to me.

For, indeed, the fourth Nirvana is that state of truth in which supreme salvation is not distinct from sorrowful transmigration, and for these blessed beings this is Nirvana; that, possessing the fullness of wisdom, they cannot desire to delay in transmigration, nor do they reënter Nirvana, because they feel the extreme of compassion for other beings.

For, in the Buddhist doctrine, compassion is the first of all virtues, and leads and is the essence of the five cardinal virtues, which are—note the sequence—pity, justice, urbanity, sincerity, *and* wise behavior. To the Buddhist, the pitiless are the ungodly. Hence the teaching of kindliness to all living beings, which is one of the "pure precepts" of the "greater vehicle," and through which all beings can obtain salvation.

For the happiness, which is the aim of Buddhism, is not limited to the individual, but is to be useful, to be of profit, to all mankind—a happiness which can only be moral, but which must act on the body as intimately as the soul is united with it.

These are the aspirations of higher Buddhism—its supreme end, to achieve the happiness of this life and of the future one—of the individual and of humanity, but differently, according to times and circumstances and human powers. In its full ideal here below civil and religious society would be the same; the continual rest of Nirvana becoming finally inseparable from our transmigrations—our passions living together with complete wisdom, and our further existence not demanding, then, another world. And if civilization shall have finally perfected the world of mind and the world of matter, we shall have here below Nirvana, and we shall dwell in it as Buddhas.

SKETCHING.—THE FLUTES OF IYÉYASŬ

IN the afternoon I go through the little road toward the west, whose walls are spotted with mosses and creepers, and where the gutters are filled with clear, noisy torrents, echoing in answer to the general sound of waters. Rarely do I meet any one—perhaps some trousered peasant girls, drowsily leading pack-horses; or naked peasants, with muscles of yellow bronze, carrying brushwood on their backs. The sun is at its hottest. Above the beat of the waters rises the perpetual strident, interminable cry of the locusts, like the shrill voice of mourners in this abode of tombs—the voice of dust and aridity. I turn a corner of high wall and tall trees and enter, through a dilapidated gateway and up some high steps in the wall, an open space, whose unknown borders are concealed behind the enormous trunks of cryptomeria. For weeks carpenters have been slowly repairing a temple building in this court, the big beams and planks of freshly-cut wood perfuming the place with the smell of cedar. In the grass and on the broken pavement lie moldering fragments of the older work, still with a waxy covering of the red lacquer which holds together the dark, dusty fibers.

A little bell-tower, lacquered red, stands near the other entrance, to which I pass. That one has its wall and high fence all lacquered red, and a gateway also red and spotted with yellow and gray mosses. Down its big steps I go, seeing just before me, through the gigantic trees and their gray and red trunks, the face of the tall pagoda, which flanks one side of the court before Iyéyasŭ, and whose other side turns toward the avenue of Iyémitsŭ. The road upon which I come is the avenue of Iyéyasŭ. Three different slopes lead within it to the paved court, where stands the high Torii of stone, through which one goes by the middle path to the high steps and the wall, the boundary of the temple. Two great banks, blocked with great dressed stones, separate the three paths — the central path being cut into wide steps which lead up to the Torii. On each of these masses of earth and masonry grow great cryptomeria trees, each of their trunks almost filling, from side to side, the entire width of the surface. They are planted irregularly. As the further ends of the banks are less high from the ground, I climb up, and sit to sketch against one of the ragged and splintered trunks. For all these late afternoons but one all has been the same. Far above me, through the needle branches of bright or shadowy green, large white clouds roll and spread in a brilliant, blotty, wet, blue sky. The court is framed in dark green, all above dazzling in light. The great Torii stands in the half shade — the edge of its upper stone shining as if gilded with yellow moss, and stains of black and white and rusty red contrasting with the delicate gilded inscriptions incised on the lower part of the two supporting columns.

Beyond, the white wall and steps of the temple inclosure are crowned with white stone palings and a red lacquer wall behind them, and the red lacquer and bronzed-roofed gateway. Here and there gold glitters on the carvings and on the ends of its many roof-beams. Near it the great gray tree-trunks are spaced, and out of the green branches shows the corner of the stable of the Sacred Horses. Its gray walls are spotted in places with gold and color. Beyond it are the red walls of one of the treasure houses; made of beams with slanting edges; and in the gable under its black eaves two symbolic animals, the elephant and the tapir, are carved and painted gray and white on the gilded wall. At this distance the bands of many-colored ornament make a glimmering of nameless color. Farther back in the trees spots of heavy black and shining gold mark the roofs of other buildings. The great trees near me almost hide the great pagoda, and I can see of it only a little red, and the green under its many eaves, which melts like a haze into the green of the trees.

All these effects of color and shape seem but as a decoration of the trees, and as modes of enhancing their height and their stillness. The great court becomes nothing but a basin with highly-finished edges, sunk into the mass of mountain greenery. The Torii, alone, stands lonely and mysterious. On the space between its upper stone beams is placed a great blue tablet with gold letters that designate the sacred posthumous name of Iyéyasŭ.

It is late in the year, and the place is no longer filled with pilgrims. I look down, occasionally, on a few stragglers who come up the steps below me—a few pilgrims in white dresses; peasants, sometimes with their children; Japanese tourists, who, even here, at home, seem out of place. This afternoon a couple of women, earnestly whispering, sailed across the court and turned the corner of the avenue of Iyémitsŭ— with toes turned in, as is the proper thing in this land of inversion. Their dresses of gray and brown and black had all the accentuated refinement of simplicity in color which is the character of good taste here, and which gives one the gentle thrill of new solutions of harmony. Our own absurdities were not unknown to them, for their velvet slits of eyes were partly hid under eye-glasses, in emulation of Boston or Germany. They might have been ladies: I am not sufficiently clear yet as to limits: perhaps they were *gei-shas*, who now, I understand, learn German and affect the intellectual look of nearsightedness. If they were, they were far above the two little creatures that posed for me yesterday—with all the

129

impatience of girls who, knowing what it was all about, still could not put up with the slow ways of European work, when their own artists would have been as agile and rapid and sketchy as themselves.

The *gei-shas* are one of the institutions of Japan,—a reminder of old, complete civilizations like that of Greece. They are, voluntarily, exiles from regular society and family, if one can speak of consent when they are usually brought up to their profession of the "gay science" from early girlhood. They cultivate singing and dancing, and often poetry, and all the accomplishments and most of the exquisite politeness of their country. They are the ideals of the elegant side of woman. To them is intrusted the entertainment of guests and the solace of idle hours. They are the *hetairai* of the old Greeks—and sometimes they are all that that name implies. But no one has the right to assume it from their profession, any more than that all liberties are bordered by possible license.

The two who consented to pose for me, at the same price and no more than I should have paid them had I called them in to entertain me and my guests with singing and dancing, were, the one a town, the other a country girl; and little by little they showed the difference, at first very slight to a foreigner, by all the many little things which obtain everywhere. It was a source of quiet amusement for me to see them posture, in what they call their dances, in the very room of our landlord the priest's house, where I have so often watched him sitting while his pupil bent over his writing, an antique picture, like so many Eastern scenes of the ideal of contemplative monastic study. But our little priest is away, on service at the temple of Iyémitsǔ, and his house is kept for him in his absence by some devout lady parishioner, who lent us the apartment more convenient than ours, and who undoubtedly shared in the amusement herself. And I asked myself if there had been a secret ceremony of purification afterwards.

I saw, too, lingering at the corner of Iyémitsŭ, the litter of a great lady, said to be the beauty of the court; but I was content to have her remain mysterious to me, and tried not to regret my indolence, when my companion twitted me with his presentation to her, and to associate her only with the clear porcelains that bear her princely name. And then, again, the priests of the temple of Iyéyasŭ came down to meet some prince, looking like great butterflies in green and yellow, and capped with their shining black hats. The youngest waved his fan at me in recognition, and gaily floated back up the high white steps and into the sunny inclosures beyond, more and more like some winged essence.

Then the temple attendants brushed with brooms the mosses of the pavement about the Torii, and the gates were closed. And I listened, until the blaze of the sun passed under the green film of the trees, to the fluting of the priests in the sanctuary on the hill. It was like a hymn to nature. The noise of the locusts had stopped for a time; and this floating wail, rising and falling in unknown and incomprehensible modulations, seemed to belong to the forest as completely as their cry. The shrill and liquid song brought back the indefinite melancholy that one has felt with the distant sound of children's voices, singing of Sundays in drowsy rhythms. But these sounds belonged to the place, to its own peculiar genius—of a lonely beauty, associated with an indefinite past, little understood; with death, and primeval nature, and final rest.

The last beams of the sunset made emerald jewels of the needles in the twigs above me—made red velvet of the powdery edges of broken bark, when the distant flutes ceased, and I left my study.

As I came out from the giant trees a great wave of the funereal song of the locusts passed through the air, leaving me suddenly in a greater silence as I came home. Then I could hear the rise and fall of the sound of our little waterfall in the garden as I stretched myself at the flattest on the mats, and Kato brought the tea and put it beside me.

SKETCHING.—THE PAGODA IN THE RAIN.

August 25.

THIS afternoon I returned to the entrance of Iyéyasŭ, and sketched under the great trees of the central avenue. The great white clouds were there again in the blue above, colored as with gold where they showed below through the trees; then they came nearer, then they melted together; then suddenly all was veiled, the rain came down in sheets, and I was glad of the refuge of the tea booths along the eastern wall. It was late, almost evening; no one there; a few pilgrims and attendants and priests scurried away through the court, disappearing with bare reddened legs and wet clogs around the corners of the avenues. And the rain persisted, hanging before me like a veil of water. I had in front, as I sat in the booths, already damp and gusty with drafts, the face of the tall red pagoda behind its stone balustrade and at right angles to the great Torii that I had been painting. The great trees were all of one green, their near and far columns flattened out with the branches into masses of equal values. Through them, below, in the few openings to the west, the sky was colored with the sunset, as if it were clear far over Nan-tai-san. The gold of the roofs' edges and of the painted carvings below was light and pale as the sky far away. Higher up the gold was bright and clear under the rain, which made it glisten; it glowed between the brackets of the lower cornices and paled like silver higher up. All the innumerable painted carvings and projections and ornaments looked pale behind the rain, while the great red mass grew richer as it rose, and

133

the bronze roofs, freshly washed, were blacker, and the green copper glistened, like malachite, on the edges of the vermilion rails, or on the bells which hung from the roof corners, against the sky or against the trees. The green, wet mosses spotted with light the stone flags below, or glowed like a fairy yellow flame on the adjoining red lacquer of the temple fence, so drenched now that I could see reflected in it the white divisions and still whiter lichens of the stone balustrade. Below it the great temple wall was blotched with dark purple and black lichens, and the columns of the Torii were white at the bottom with mosses. Its upper cross-arm glistened yellow with their growths as if it had caught the sun. But the heavy rain was drenching all; and now from all the roofs of the pagoda poured lines of water, the one within the other, the highest describing a great curve that encircled all the others, and the whole high tower itself, as if with a lengthened aureole of silver drops. It was as if water had poured out from the fountain basins, one above the other, which the Italian Renaissance liked to picture on tall pilasters, even as this one was profiled against the sky and distant rain. Below, a yellow torrent covered the great court with an eddying lake, and its course rushed down the great steps or made a crested, bounding line along the gutters by the walls. I watched for a time the beautiful curves dropping from the roofs of the tower, until all grew dark and my coolie arrived to carry paint box and easel, and we managed to get home, with sketching umbrellas, wet, however, through every layer of clothing.

FROM NIKKO TO KAMAKURA

NIKKO, August 27.

YESTERDAY, I went out in another afternoon of blazing sunlight, up to the corner of the temple inclosure and along its outside edge, where the rocks of the mountain, covered with trees, make a great vague wall. Under the damp trees runs a path paved with small blocks of stone, slippery with moss, or, when bare, smoothed by ages of treading. This road leads to the little cascade which supplies the sacred water-tank of the temple of Iyéyasŭ, that square block of water under the gilded and painted canopy in the great court-yard.

The waterfall drops over rocks into a hollow between the hills; high trees stand along its edge near a black octagonal shrine, with great roof, green and yellow with moss. On this side of the water, a diminutive shrine, red-painted, with columns and architrave of many colors and a roof of thatch all green, out of which are growing the small stems of young trees. In front, a Torii, just tall enough to pass under, of gray stone, all capped and edged with green, velvety moss. A curved stone, cushioned with moss, in front of it, spans the water-course that gives escape to the waters of the pool. The doors of the shrine are closed, as if to make more solitary yet the quiet of the little hollow.

Higher up, past the black building and above high steps, on a platform edged by walls, stand black buildings, shrines of Buddhist divinities, whose golden bodies I can see through the grating of the unfastened doors. I feel their amiable presence, while I sit painting in the damp sunlight, and the murmur of the waters seems their whispered encouragement.

On my return I looked again toward the abrupt rocky hill to find a little monument we had passed at its foot, just off the road. Through the inevitable Torii a little path of rough flagging, all broken up and imbedded in moss, leads across the small bridge of two large stones, one of whose parapets is gone, and up high steps, half natural, to a little altar of big stones with a heavy balustrade around three sides. A little stone shrine with a roof stands upon it, and behind it a tall gray rock upon which is incised and gilded a device of five disks forming a circle. All around about the path and shrine are trees covered with moss; the rocks, the shrine, the path, are spotted with green and yellow velvet; all looks as if abandoned to nature,—all but the gilded armorial bearings in the mossy stone, which I take to be those of the divinized mortal in whose honor this little record has been built, Tenjin Sama, known and worshiped by every schoolboy in Japan. He is the patron of learning and of penmanship, and was during his life a great scholar and minister of state under the name of Michizane. This was just before the year nine hundred. A faithful minister, a learned and just man, he naturally gave great umbrage, especially to a younger associate whose sister was Empress, and who succeeded through malicious slander in bringing about Michizane's banishment.

In his place of exile, separated from wife and children, he died two years later. There, I suppose, he rode about on the saddled bull, upon which Yosai has placed him in his drawings, as also he was seen by Motonobu in a dream, of which I have a drawing. There the great artist has represented him, faithful, I suppose, to what he really saw, as a younger man than he really could have been, galloping swiftly and bending down to avoid the branches of the trees above.

Bulls of bronze and marble adorn his temple in Kioto, recalling how the bull that drew him to the cemetery refused to go further than a certain spot, where he was buried in a grave dug hastily. Misfortune and remorse followed his enemies, with the death of the Imperial heir; so that the Emperor, revoking his banishment, reinstalled the dead man in the honors of his office, and bestowed a high rank upon his ghost. Since then his worship has grown, as I said above.

As you see, the Mikado has been the fountain of honor for this world and the next; and I cannot help being reminded of the constant relations of Chinese and Japanese thought in this unity — this constant joining of that which we separate. The forms of China may be more "bureaucratic"; no such national prejudices and feelings can belong to the idea of the sovereign there as must exist in Japan, with a dynasty of rulers as Japanese as Japan itself. But there has been here, as there, a sort of natural duty in the Government to look after all the relations of those intrusted to its care. In China, all religion or religions must depend upon the sanction of the ruling powers; nothing is too great or too small to be satisfied with; official approval may attend the worship of some local heroine, official disapproval may be shown to some exaggerations of Taoist superstitions. The source of this right and this duty is always the idea that in the ruler all is centered; he is responsible to Heaven, and is the tie between the powers above and the deities below. Hence there is nothing absurd in his following the governed after death.

In Japan, the forms of this power may be different, but its workings will be similar, and hero-worship, combined with the respect and worship of ancestors, has had a most important part in the development of life here, in encouraging patriotism and lofty ideas, and in stimulating the chivalrous

137

feeling, the ideas of honor, that seem to me the peculiar note of the Japanese. However misapplied, however unfamiliar some forms of these ideas may appear to us, I cannot make for myself a definition of the national character, nor see a clue to many of their actions unless I bear in mind the ruling power of this feeling. While we are in this place, where Iyéyasŭ's name is so important, let me cite a trifling anecdote.

It is said that on some occasion he accompanied Hideyoshi, the great Taiko Sama, each with few attendants, upon some visit, and all were afoot. Now, among the retinue of Iyéyasŭ was one Honda, a man of preternatural strength, who hinted to his master that this might be an opportunity for an attack upon his great rival. But Taiko guessed the danger, and, turning round, said to Iyéyasŭ: "My sword is heavy, for me unaccustomed to walking, so may I not ask your servant to carry it for me?" For Taiko knew that it would have been considered a disgrace to attack a man unarmed when he had intrusted his sword, not to his own servant, but to the servant of his enemy. And Iyéyasŭ understood this appeal to the idea of honor.

August 28.

Two more days and we shall be gone. As I sketch in the temples or about them, everything seems more beautiful as it grows to be more a part of my daily existence. Though I am perpetually harassed through feeling that I cannot copy everything, and through trying to force my memory to grasp so as to retain the multitudinous details of the architectural decoration, I have drawn the curve of this, and the patterns of that, and noted the colors, but I wonder, if the thread gets loosened that holds them together, whether I shall ever be able to separate one from another in their entanglement. And then I still do not wish to work. There are so many places that I should like to look at again without the oppression of an obligatory record.

138

This evening I must take another look at the neglected graves of the followers of Iyémitsŭ who committed suicide, as my Japanese account has it, "that they might accompany him in his dark pilgrimage to the future world." At least it says this of Hotta Masemori and of three others; while the graves, as I remember them, are twenty-one in number, and about this I have never thought to ask, but I must do so. And then there may have been retainers of retainers. It is a pleasure to me anyhow to set down at least one name and to help to keep this memory clear when I think of the neglected spot in which they lie. It is not far from that part of the land where stood the residence of their master's family, now destroyed, through the days of turbulence which closed the last moments of their reign. Broken fragments of fencing still lean against the little inclosures of stone posts, balustrade, and gate that surround each memorial pillar. They stand in two rows in a little clearing, the valley sunk behind them, hidden in part by much wild growth.

O—— was telling us some little while ago of the feudal habit which gave to a chieftain the vow of certain retainers who undertook to follow him faithfully even beyond the grave. It was expected of them in war that they should be about him sharing in his struggle, and if he died in peace, near or far, they should be ready to go too.

And as death is the most important thing in life, I cannot help thinking over the condition of mind of any one who looked forward to such a limitation of its lease.

When age had changed the view of life, had created more ties, more duties, had made the term nearer and more capricious, while everything else became more fixed, did this bond, with its promise of payment to be met at any moment's demand, become a heavy burden of debt? I can occasionally conjure up a picture—perhaps erroneous, because my imagination of the circumstances may displace them,—of some older man settled in pleasant places, rested in secure possessions, with dependants, with friends, with affections around his life, learning at any moment of the probability that the call might come. He might be summoned from any festivity or joy as if by a knocking at the door. How curiously he must have watched the runners of the mail who might be bringing into his town the news from the court, or whereso-ever this other life—which to all purposes was his own—was perhaps ebbing away. How then he would have known what to do, even to its most minute detail, and be but part of a ceremonial that he himself would direct. Vague memories come up to me of places set apart in the garden, and the screens and the hangings and the lights that belonged to the voluntary ordeal. But as I keep on thinking, I feel more certain that my fancy displaces the circumstances of former times and of a different civilization. For instance, the concentration of the feudal territory, habits of clanship, the constant attendance, must have narrowed the circle and made the individual more like a part of one great machinery, one great family, than he can ever be again. The weakness, the insufficiency of the individual, has been stiffened by the importance of the family, of the clan, as a basis of society; and I could almost say that I discern in this one main-spring of the peculiar courtesy of this nation, which seems to go along with a great feeling of a certain freedom, so that the obedience of the inferior does not seem servile. The servant who has done his duty of respectful service seems afterward ready to take any natural relation that may turn up. The youth trained in respect to his betters and elders, and silent in their presence, will give his opinion frankly when asked, with a want of diffidence quite unexpected. The coming years are certain to bring changes that cannot be arrested.

.   .   .   .   .

While I was being baked to-day, at my work that I could

not leave, my companions have been away on a visit higher up the mountains, to the hot baths on the lake, and, at least for part of the time, have had the weather almost cold. They have much to say about the baths, and the fullness of visitors, and the difficulty of getting place, and one of them has gone to her bath in the native dress, and another cannot yet quite get over the impression made upon him by the pretty young lady near whom he stood under the eaves of the bath-house, where he had taken refuge from the rain, and whose modest manners were as charming as her youthfulness, and had no more covering.

Here everything is still hot and damp, though our nights are cooler and I am able to make out more conveniently my notes and my sketches and my memoranda of purchased acquisitions. On the lower floor boxes are being filled, and to-morrow evening horses and men will stand in our garden to be laden; we shall follow the light of their lanterns down the road, and they will seem to be carrying parts of us away from Nikko.

NIKKO TO YOKOHAMA

NEAR UTSUNOMIYA, August 30.

WE left Nikko this morning; a hot, moist, quiet, lovely morning. We dawdled at our friends' house and breakfasted, and said good-by to our worthy landlord. Yesterday he had found fault with my sketching him in his ordinary yellow priest's dress, while he had vestments as beautiful as any painter or clergyman could desire; in proof of which he had rushed into his house and reappeared in those lovely things and moved about the green of the garden looking as radiant as any flamingo. But I knew not of these possessions of his, and regretted quite as deeply as he could himself not having painted him in them.

It was a sad moment—that of leaving his little garden for good, and walking down the road to the enormous steps under the trees by the river, where we reversed the picture of our arrival six weeks ago. There stood the naked runners, and our hostess above us, as we sat in the *kurumas*, but this time the doctor was not with us, except to bid us good-by. His place was filled by the professional guide and factotum, who sat anxious for departure in his own *kuruma*, and who for days had been packing and labeling and helping to make lists, and receiving instructions, and bustling about at times when he was not sleeping—and generally making life a misery. We rattled over the bridge, passed the children going to school, and the polite policeman with spectacles and sword, who looks like a German Rath of some kind or other, and the

142

woman of the Eta class [1] who has sold us skins of monkeys and of badgers, as well as two baby monkeys, whom we have disrespectfully named Sesson and Sosen, after the painters who so beautifully portrayed their ancestors.

Soon we had entered the long avenue of cryptomeria and kept on through shadow and sunlight, with our runners at their fullest gait, for we had to be in time for the afternoon train at Utsunomiya, and it is twenty-two miles from Nikko. But we were more than in time, and had to wait at an inn near the station. I am absurdly stupid and fatigued, so that I have given up watching the landscape and merely make these notes. Besides, there is a missionary near us so self-contented that I feel like withdrawing into my own self and dreaming of the times he was not here. I recall a little story of Utsunomiya, connected with my associations of Nikko, which I shall try to tell you; though, at the very start, I find a difficulty in my having heard it told in several different and contradictory ways—and I can only travel one at a time. As I shall tell it, it represents a legend believed at least in the theater, which, as we know, everywhere makes a kind of history.

The story is about the shogun Iyémitsŭ, whose temple, you know, is at Nikko, and who was near missing the honour of being divinized there later, owing to a plot arranged by his enemies, the scene of which was this little town of Utsunomiya. At that time he was but a boy, the heir-apparent, and was on his way to Nikko, as was his official duty, to worship at the tomb of his grandfather Iyéyasŭ, lately deceased. In this story Iyémitsu is not in the legitimate line

[1] "Pariahs. Their occupations were to slaughter animals, tan leather, attend at executions, etc. The class, as such, is now abolished, but remnants of its peculiar dress may still occasionally be seen in the persons of young girls with broad hats who go about the streets playing and singing." (Satow).

of descent, but is made the heir by the decision of the great Iyéyasŭ.

His father, Hidetada, was shogun, as you know, having succeeded Iyéyasŭ, during the latter's lifetime,—the old man remaining in reality the master, though absolved from external responsibilities. Now, Hidetada's wife was of the family of Nobunaga, on her mother's side—and bore him a son, who was named during his childhood Kuni Matsu. Another son, whose boy name was Take Chiyo, was the son of Kasuga No Tsubone, a remarkable woman. Each son had tutors, people of importance, and around each boy gathered a number of ambitious interests, all the fiercer that they were dissembled and depended for success upon the choice of either heir as shogun, to succeed father and grandfather. The claim of the other son was favored by the father and more generally accepted; but the son of Kasuga was superior in looks, manners, and intelligence, and his mother hoped to influence in his favor old Iyéyasŭ, the grandfather.

Iyéyasŭ was then living in retirement at Sunpu, that is now called Shidzuoka, which is on the road called the Tokaido.

Kasuga took advantage of a pilgrimage to the shrines of Ise to stop on her road, and naturally offer homage to the head of the family, the grandfather of her son. Besides the power of her own personality, she was able to place before Iyéyasŭ very strong arguments for choosing as the heir of the line a youth as promising as her Take Chiyo.

Iyéyasŭ advised her to continue her pilgrimage, and not to go out of her woman's business, which could not be that of interfering with questions of state; and she obeyed. But Iyéyasŭ revolved the entire question in his mind, and decided that there was danger in a delay that allowed both parties to grow stronger in antagonism. So that he came at once to Yedo, which is now Tokio, and visited Hidetada, asking to see both the boys together. They came in along with their father and his wife, and took their accustomed places. Now these were on the higher floor, raised by a few inches from the floor on which kneels the visitor of lower degree, in the presence of his superior: a line of black lacquer edges the division. Thereupon Iyéyasŭ taking the boy Take Chiyo by the hand, made him sit by him, and alongside of his father, and ordered the other son, Kuni Matsu, to sit below the line, and said: "The State will come to harm if the boys are allowed to grow up in the idea of equal rank. Therefore, Take Chiyo shall be shogun, and Kuni Matsu a daimio." This decision gave to the line of the Tokugawa a brilliant and powerful continuity, for Take Chiyo, under his manhood name of Iyémitsŭ, was as an Augustus to the Cæsar Iyéyasŭ. And, indeed, Iyéyasŭ had certainly made sufficient inquiries to warrant his decision. If he consulted the abbot Tenkai, of Nikko, who was a preceptor of the boy, he must have heard favorably of him. For, according to the judgment of Tenkai, as I find it quoted elsewhere, "Iyémitsŭ was very shrewd and of great foresight," and in his presence the great abbot felt, he said, "as if thorns were pricking his back."

Not but that he was also fond of luxury and splendor; and one glimpse of him as a youth shows a quarrel with a tutor who found him dressing himself, or being dressed, for "No" performances, or "private theatricals," and who proceeded thereupon to throw away the double mirrors,—in which the youth followed his hair-dresser's arrangements,—with the usual, classical rebuke, condemning such arrangements as unworthy of a ruler of Japan.

There are many stories of Iyémitsŭ more or less to his advantage—and a little anecdote shows a young man of quick temper, as well as one who insisted upon proper attendance.

Iyémitsŭ had been hawking in a strong wind, and with no success. Tired and hungry, he went with some lord-in-waiting to a neighboring temple, where lunch was prepared for them by his cook, — a man of rank. Iyémitsŭ, while taking his soup in a hurry, crushed a little stone between his teeth: whereupon he immediately insisted upon the cook's committing suicide. The cook being a gentleman, a man of affairs, not a mere artist like poor Vatel, hesitated, and then said: "No soup made by me ever had stones or pebbles in it; otherwise I should gladly kill myself: you gentlemen have begun dinner at once without washing hands or changing dress, and some pebble has dropped into the soup from your hair or clothes. If, after having washed your hands and changed your dress, you find any stones in the soup, I shall kill myself." Whereupon Iyémitsŭ did as was suggested by the cook, repented of his own severity, and increased the cook's pay. But the tutor and guardians of Iyémitsŭ watched over him carefully, and the story I had begun to tell shows that they had no sinecure.

The tutors and guardians of the brother, whom Iyéyasŭ had decided to put aside in favor of Iyémitsŭ, were naturally deeply aggrieved and sought for chances to regain their ward's future power and their own.

As my story began, Iyémitsŭ, representing the hereditary shogunate, was called upon to travel to Nikko and worship officially at his grandfather's tomb. On his way it was natural that he should rest as we did, at Utsunomiya, and in the castle of his vassal, Honda, who was one of the tutors of his brother. This was the son of the great Honda Masanobu, of whom I spoke above as a champion of Iyéyasŭ.

Here was an opportunity; and a scheme of getting rid of the young shogun was devised by his enemies that seemed to them sufficiently obscure to shield them in case of success or failure, at least for a time. This was, to have a movable ceiling made to the bath-room weighted in such a way as to fall upon any one in the bath and crush him.

Whether it was to be lifted again, and leave him drowned in his bath, or to remain as an accident from faulty construction, I do not know.

To build this machine, ten carpenters were set to work within the castle and kept jealously secluded,—even when the work was done, for the young shogun delayed his coming. This confinement fretted the men, among whom was a young lover, anxious to get back to his sweetheart, and not to be satisfied with the good food and drink provided to appease him. He told of his longings to the gatekeeper, whose duty it was to keep him imprisoned, bribed him with his own handsome pay and promise of a punctual return, and at last managed to get out and be happy for a few moments. The girl of his love was inquisitive, but reassured by explanation that the work was done, and that he should soon be out again; yet not before the shogun should have come and gone on his way to Nikko. And so he returned to the gatekeeper at the time appointed. Meanwhile, during that very night, the officers of the castle had gone their rounds and found one man absent. In the morning the roll-call was full. This was reported to the lord of the castle, who decided that if he could not know who it was that had been absent it was wise to silence them all. Therefore, each was called to be paid and dismissed, and, as he stepped out, was beheaded. The gatekeeper, getting wind of what was happening and fearing punishment, ran away, and being asked by the girl about her lover, told her what he knew and that he believed all the carpenters to have been killed.

Since her lover was dead, she determined to die also, having been the cause of his death and of the death of his companions. She wrote out all this, together with what her lover had told her of his belief and suspicions, and left the letter for her father and mother, who received it along with the tidings of her suicide. The father, in an agony of distress

147

and fear, for there was danger to the whole family from every side, made up his mind to stop the shogun at all hazards, and in the depth of the night made his way to Ishibashi, where one of the princes had preceded Iyémitsŭ, who was to pass the night still further back on the road.

Here there was difficulty about getting a private interview with so great a man as this prince, whose name you will remember as being the title of the former owner of our friend's house in Nikko: Ii, Kammon no Kami.

The letter was shown to Ii, who despatched two messengers, gentlemen of his own, one back to Yedo, to see to the safety of the castle there; the other one to Iyémitsŭ, but by a circuitous route, so that he might appear to have come the other way. The letter was to the effect that the young shogun's father was very ill and desired his son's immediate return. By the time that Iyémitsŭ could get into his litter, Ii had arrived and shown him the girl's letter. Then the occupants of the litters were changed, Matsudaira taking Iyémitsŭ's *norimono* and Iyémitsŭ Matsudaira's. This, of course, was to give another chance of escape in case of sudden attack by a larger force, for they were now in enemy's country and did not know what traps might be laid for them. The bearers of the palanquin pressed through the night, so that, leaving at midnight, they arrived at Yedo the following evening; but the strain had been so great that they could go no further. There was still the fear of attack, and among the retinue one very strong man, Matsudaira Ishikawa, carried the litter of the prince himself. But the gates were closed, and the guards refused to recognize the unknown litter as that of the shogun; nor would they, fearing treachery, open when told that Iyémitsŭ had returned. Delays ensued, but at last admission was obtained for Iyémitsŭ through a wicket gate — and he was safe. Later, after cautious delays, the guilty were punished, and I hope the family of the carpenter's love escaped. When I first read the story, years ago, the version was different, and there was some arrangement of it, more romantic—with some circumstances through which the young carpenter and his sweetheart escaped, and alone the father, innocent of harm, committed suicide. The story sounded sufficiently Japanese and upside down and was pretty, but I have forgotten its convolutions, so that I give you this one, which I think has a pleasant local color. It has local color, and that charm of action which belongs to such histories as those of the great Dumas—not to mention Mr. Froude.

Do not forget that these details are given for your amusement, and not for your instruction. I am quite uncertain as to the historical value of my information as soon as I come down to close particulars. What little I really know comes down from early reading of the missionaries and of the Dutch, and that is mostly outside impression, though thereby valuable, because not based on theory or principle.

I do not know that critical history has yet begun here. But in the historical place where we have spent our summer, talk about the past was but natural and all to be listened to without much chance for us to distinguish what was of record and what was of legend. What I have been writing about is legend, and I am warned of its complicated incorrectness. That has not prevented my setting it down. You would like the pretty murderous story whose details reflect a peculiar past. It would be nothing to you if it were not at all Iyémitsǔ, but his father Hidetada, for whose destruction the famous plot of the Hanging Ceiling was hatched. Nor would you care if the ceiling and bath-room had never existed. What is worth having is that many people thought that they saw themselves in the mirror of a period.

Now see how re-arranging the atoms of which the previous story is constituted will give you quite another picture that I would spare you, though it is a correct historical one, but it has the advantage of being quite as strange in certain ways, though not so fitted for the theater, and of giving you again a picture of feudal Japan.

As I said before, the story as I have just told it has been kept in memory, if not invented on purpose, through a book written in honor of a Japanese opposed to Honda, the master of the castle, the author of the plot of the Hanging Ceiling. There may have been such a story afloat at that time among people of low degree kept out from the many secrets of the court, but knowing that things were being done; at the same time, there is nothing that would account for a sufficient reason; and, worse than all, the date is impossible. Young Iyémitsŭ was not in any position at that possible date (eighth year of the Genwa) to represent the shogunate. His father Hidetada would have been the proposed victim, which is again impossible because of the devotion of Honda, the lord of the castle, to Hidetada. That there was such an accusation I believe is understood. It was met at the time and at once disproved to the satisfaction of the shogun. It was the Lady Kano who had denounced Honda, and apparently invented the plot. She was a daughter of Iyéyasŭ, and had, perhaps, some of the fierce strain said to have shown in her mother and sister. Her baby grandson had only just been deprived of this very fief for the advantage of Honda, so that she had at least this grievance. And she was united in intention with the wife of the shogun Hidetada. This was a beautiful and wilful woman,—known to us by her after-death name of Sogenin, whose preference for Iyémitsŭ's brother, her son also, had met Honda's resistance. You can realize that I am not capable of even discussing the question, and that I am only doing it to amuse you and to bring in more pictures.

As the shogun was to be received by the lord of Utsuno-miya, new additions were ordered for his castle, the bridges and roads were repaired, which works required all the laborers, skilled or otherwise, of his domains, and even obliged him to draw upon his retainers and soldiers. Such enormous preparations were, of course, noised abroad. Now, it so happened that at one time Honda's father had been concerned in an insurrection, or levy of arms, of certain members of the Buddhist sect to which he belonged, and had fought the great Iyéyasŭ, whom afterwards he served so faithfully. Among the upholders of the faith were fighting monks, a variety of the militant church well known in the annals of Japan. At the close of this rebellion a band of these monks—something like a hundred—and a hundred other warriors were intrusted—Japanese-way—to the wardship of their former fellow partisan, and there they were handy for use. But they had retained something of both the clergyman and the warrior, keeping their priestly names and wearing their hair unshorn, and they refused to work, which in their eyes would have assimilated them to common soldiers and laborers. Thereupon,—and this was thought to be queer even in those days,—the lord of the castle invited them to go about the country and report upon certain matters in various places, at which places they were met by bodies of armed men, who put an end to them. I suppose that, according to strict views of the country and time, this was justifiable, though excessive, and this is one of the little pictures that I wish to frame. You see how the unpleasantness of the occasion might help the later stories of assassination.

And now, in correcting another error, I can give you another picture of feudal Japan, a Japan now broken up, against whose last rulers, the Tokugawa, I hear daily so much. That lady in the story just given you, where she is the mother of Iyémitsŭ and the concubine of his father, the shogun, was a very different person.

Little Iyémitsŭ was the legitimate son; moreover, the one who by date of birth was the probable heir, notwithstanding the preference shown by his father and his mother, Sogenin, for his younger brother. So that the succession was decided abruptly by the stern head of the family, Iyéyasŭ.

Great attention was paid by the grandfather, the great Iyéyasŭ, to the education of this grandson. As a Japanese friend remarked, he believed that the important place in the generation was that of the third man. So that three distinguished noblemen were appointed his governors: Sakai, to teach benevolence; Doi, to teach wisdom; Awoyama, to teach valor. Besides these great professors for the future, the little boy needed an immediate training by a governess good in every way. Kasuga, a married woman, the daughter of a well-known warrior of imperial descent who had lost his life in some conspiracy of the previous generation, was chosen by the government for the position. This was, perhaps, as great an honor as could be offered to any lady. Besides, there was an opportunity to clear the memory of her father. And she begged her husband to divorce her that she might be free to give all her life to this task. So devoted was she that the boy being at one time at the point of death, she offered herself to the gods for his recovery, vowing never to take any remedy. In her last illness she refused all medicine, and even when Iyémitsŭ—now ruler—begged her to take a commended draught from his hand, she merely, out of politeness, allowed it to moisten her lips, saying that her work was done, that she was ready to die, and that her life had long ago been offered for the master. Nor would she allow the master to indulge her with regard to her own son. He was in exile, deservedly, and the shogun asked her permission to pardon him, in the belief of possible amendment. She refused, bidding Iyémitsŭ to remember his lesson: that the law of the country was above all things, and that she had never expected such words from him. Moreover, that had he revoked the law for her, she could not die in peace. There is a Spartan politeness in all this, for which I think the stories worth saving to you.

And they will help to give Iyémitsŭ existence for you. He seems too vague in the temple dedicated to him at Nikko, even when we look at his bronze tomb and are told that he lies there packed in vermilion: our minds have become so far removed from the ways of thinking of Japan that a divinized mortal is an empty phrase for us.

The details of such stories as I have told would not have seemed very antiquated across the seas, at their date, to those who remembered the days of Queen Elizabeth. The change has been as great in Europe as in Japan, but here it has been sudden, like the shifting of the scene of the theater; so that I can realize that when I was a boy such things as I am telling you would not have seemed very old-fashioned hereabouts.

And now I make my notes in this little railroad coach, with the telegraph wires running in and out of the picture that I see through my window; and, indeed, it is this implied contrast which I think has urged me most to tell you these more or less accurate anecdotes.

If you wished to learn more about Iyémitsŭ from the Japanese biography that I have with me, you might be puzzled. One has felt so distinctly the all-powerfulness of the men whose names and stories are the outer history of Japan. So full is the impression forced upon one by the outside of the life of such a ruler as Iyémitsŭ, bounded between the worship of his grandfather in golden temples and his own worship in almost equal splendors, and filled in by despotic use of power, that it leaves little place for the theory of all this power coming from the Mikado, who practically lived upon a narrow income apportioned to him by his lieutenant, the shogun. But in my little biography, written evidently to keep to present views and theories, I learn that toward the emperor our impatient hero was "faithful and humble"— and part of his story consists of visits to the emperor and of his receiving honors from this source of all honor. Thus, upon his coming of age, and having his hair trimmed, cut, and shaved in a manner to indicate this important event, the emperor sends a great court officer to compliment him, gives him the name of Iyémitsŭ, honors him with the rank of *Junii*, and appoints him a Go Dainagon. Also, later he appoints him to be the commander of the right wing of the imperial guard, and also superintendent of the Right Imperial Stable. Thereupon Iyémitsŭ calls upon his majesty at Kioto to pay his homage, and is made commander-in-chief of the army and navy, and moreover Naidaizin, with the rank of Shonii; and he is also permitted to ride in an ox-carriage and to have armed body-guards; the latter privilege one that he had been obliged to enjoy perforce from early days, as we have seen. Whereupon, says my chronicler, Iyémitsŭ had the honor of presenting to his majesty a yearly income of twenty thousand bags of rice; and this goes on until after his death, when the emperor gives him these titles for the future, the name of Daiken-In, the rank of Shoichi, and the premier office of Daijo-Daizin. "The favor of Five Imperial poems was also extended to the deceased."

Iyémitsŭ was fond of painting, and studied under the instruction of Kano Tanyu. He liked to paint the sacred mountain Fuji, and the same courteous chronicler tells me that some of his work was better than Tanyu's. But I should prefer seeing, before deciding; though Tanyu's imperturbable security makes one not a little bored.

It is dark; we are approaching Iyémitsŭ's city, Tokio, formerly Yedo, the city of the Tokugawa, now finally returned to the emperor, to whom they gave the thousands of bags of rice for income. We shall sleep at No. 22 Yokohama,[1] and look out on the water again.

[1] All of Yokohama given to foreign settlement was laid out by numbering, and retains it, apart from any other designation.

YOKOHAMA—KAMAKURA

Yokohama, September 1, 1886.

NATURALLY we have again been wandering in Tokio; I don't know that we have seen anything more, as we should certainly do if we had any energy in the heat. It is more natural to fritter away time in little things. Besides, there is a general feeling of discouragement accompanying the continuance of cholera; and this is an unseasonable moment. Theaters are closed; people are away. If I had to give an account of my time, I could not make it up. I know that I went to see an engraver on wood; that he showed me his work, or his way of working, of which I knew a little; that he made me drink some cherry-blossom tea, pretty to look at and of unseizable flavor; that he took me to see some of his work printed; that I climbed up a ladder, somewhere into a hot room, where a man, naked but for his loin-cloth, sat slapping pieces of paper with a big brush upon the block previously touched with color; and that the dexterity with which he fitted the paper in proper place, so that the colors should not overlap, was as simple and primitive as his dress.

Then I went to see the painter whose drawings had been engraved. I can't explain just why the arrangement of his courtyard seemed what I might have expected, and yet I still keep that impression without having noticed anything but the heat—the heat and the sun—the heat accumulated in this big dreary city of innumerable little houses.

We explained at the door our request, and after a few

moments we were told that the painter, though he was ill, would see us. We entered, and sat awhile, during which interval a boy pupil, occupied in copying sketches of the master, looked at us surreptitiously through a circular opening in the partition that made him a room.

Our artist came in and sat down, evidently an ill man, and offered us the inevitable tea, and showed us his methods of preparation for the colored wood-blocks, and got down examples from the great pile of rolls and bundles of papers and drawings that filled one side of the room, among which I noticed many fragments of illustrated English or American newspapers. And we dared not intrude any further, and departed—just as the conversation had turned toward European art—with gifts of drawings from him and promise of exchange.

No; what we have really done is again to call at shops and begin over again the pursuit of bric-à-brac. It is so impossible to believe that we can find nothing in all the accumulation of all these shops. But even if it be so, the manner of hunting is an amusement, as is the mere seeing of all this stuff in its own home; and the little attentions of the dealer, the being in a house with the privileges of tea and smoking, and a lazy war of attack and defense; and the slow drawing out of pieces from bags and boxes, so that time, the great enemy, is put in the wrong. And then, what one is not expected to buy or look at is quite as good. I know of one place to which I have returned to look out of the *shoji* screens into the garden, where there is a big pottery statue of Kwannon. I don't intend to get it or to bargain about it, but I intend to buy other things under its influence; perhaps the *daimio* seats that we use in our visit, or the lanterns that light us when we stay late, whose oil will have to be emptied if they are sold. And there are places where things are for sale to people versed in Chinese ways of thinking, but where amateurs on the wing like ourselves are not encouraged, and that is certainly seductive. Still, I am afraid that we shall miss a great deal that we wish to see, because of this dawdling in shops.

And yet there is no sadness following these visits, such as has come upon us when we have gone to see some of the modern workers. From them we depart with no more hope. It is like some puzzles, like the having listened to an argument which you know is based on some inaccuracy that you cannot at the moment detect. This about the better, the new perfect work, if I can call it perfect, means only high finish and equal care. But the individual pieces are less and less individual; there is no more *surprise*. The means or methods are being carried further and *beyond*, so that one asks one's self, "Then why these methods at all?" The *style* of this finer modern work is poorer, no longer connected with the greater design, as if ambition was going into method and value of material. Just how far this is owing to us I cannot tell, but the market is largely European, and what is done has a vague appearance of looking less and less out of place among our works, and has, as I said before, less and less suggestion of individuality. None of it would ever give one the slight shock of an exception, none of it would have the appearance which we know of our own best work, the *feeling* that we are not going to see more of it. This statement applies to the best work; the more common work is merely a degradation, the using of some part of the methods; just enough to sell it, and to meet some easily defined immediate commercial needs. I saw the beginnings years ago, and I can remember one of our great New York dealers marking on his samples the colors that pleased most of his buyers, who themselves again were to place the goods in Oshkosh or Third Avenue. All other colors or patterns were tabooed in his instructions to the makers in Japan. This was the rude mechanism of the change, the coming down to the worst public taste, which must be that of the greatest number at any given time; for commerce in such matters is of the moment: the sale of the wooden nutmeg, good enough until used. Have I not seen through the enormous West any amount of the worst stained glass, all derived from what I made myself, some years ago, as a step toward a development of greater richness and delicacy in the "art of glass"? And my rivalry of precious stones had come to this ignoble end and caricature. The commercial man, or the semi-professional man whom we call the architect, must continually ask for something poorer, something to meet the advancing flood of clients and purchasers, something more easily placed anywhere, at random, without trouble or responsibility, and reflecting the public—as it is more easy to fit in a common tile than the most beautiful Persian one—in the average of buildings made themselves to meet the same common demand. And so with all applied beauty; the degradation is always liable to occur.

Japan is an exceptional place for studying these changes; we can see them gradually evolved—all as if by vivisection of some morbid anatomy. The study of these diseases and infections of art at home is attended with moral distress and intellectual disgust, because we are all in part responsible; but here we can see it disinterestedly, and speculate dispassionately upon the degradation of good things resulting from the demands of business.

Were it quite in the line of what you expect to-day from me, I might make out for you the lines of the old scheme of civilization under which former work was done. The feudal organization of Japan divided the country into provinces of distinct habits and modes of work—more or less isolated, partly by want of easy or general communication, partly by the political interests of their rulers and of the main government, partly by the permanence of the provincial feeling which prevented the inhabitant of one place moving to another to find occupation and employment. The rule of the idea of the family, which is still great in Japan, kept things in the same order, preserved all traditions, and at the same time offered opportunities, by adoption, to individuals who might increase or keep up the family reputation or influence. Here, too, I suppose, is the basis of a certain dignity and personal independence in the manners of the people which runs in with their courtesy. Every one must have known what was expected of him, and have felt quite free after that duty paid. Within this courtesy that I see all about me, I feel something of what we might call democratic, for want of a better name. I recognize it in the manner of the subordinate, who takes an apparently personal interest in things, after his duty of politeness and obedience is paid. And though there was no absolute caste, as we understand it, except in such a case as that of the Eta, the lines of life were strictly laid out, until the new laws, which have made things open more or less to all.[1] With these changes, with disturbances of fortune, with the loss of power and of income on the part of the small rulers, with a country all laid out now in "prefectures," with the necessarily increasing power of "bureaucracy," the whole tone of individual life must change, must become less independent in any one thing, more independent apparently in general—must flatten out, if I may so express it. And the artisan will have to follow the course of trade and its fluctuations until some general level has been established—some general level of manufactures, I mean, for there is no general level possible in art. Something will happen which will resemble the ways of France, where art still exists, but where things have been so managed that any

[1] The gentry, the old Samurai, however, still constitute the governing class to-day apparently, and the aristocratic spirit stands in the way of indiscriminate rise of the plebeians.

artist out of the general level has had a very bad time of it—
the whole live forces of the nation, in trade and "bureaucracy," being against his living easily any life of his own.
When the forces of traditional taste and skill and habits of
industry now existing in Japan shall have been organized
anew, Japan, like France, will have undoubtedly a great part
to play in industrial trade.

Art may live or may not in the future here; nothing of what
has been done elsewhere to grow it or foster it has made it
stronger. It has always come by the grace of God, to be
helped when it is here, or choked out; but no gardener has
ever seen its seed. Some of my friends in Japan are plunged
in a movement to save what there is of the past in art, to keep
its traditions, to keep teaching in the old ways, without direct
opposition to what may be good in the new. They see around
them the breaking up of what has been fine, and the new
influences producing nothing, not even bad imitations of
Europe. I know too little upon what their hopes are based,
but O——, who is in the "tendency," sails with us for Ameri-
ca and Europe, and I may find out more through him.
Meanwhile he is to inquire with Professor F—— into the
education of the artist and artisan with us, and to see "how
we do it." I am deeply interested in their undertaking,
perhaps the most remarkable of all similar inquiries—if
honestly conducted. But I see vague visions of distorted
values, of commercial authorities looked upon as artistic, of
the same difficulties, for instance, that I might meet if I
wished now to make an official report, not to the public or to
government,—that is always easy,—but to myself, who have
no special interest in being misled, of the methods of art and
industry that have been and exist in the East.

. . . Three days are wasted. I do scarcely any work,
and there comes to me, as a punishment, a feeling of the
littleness of a great deal here, coming, I think, from the

actual smallness of many details—the sizes of the little houses, of the little gardens, of the frail materials, of the set manners.

. . . To-morrow we shall go to something great, to the great statue, the "Daibutsŭ," at Kamakura, and perhaps we may even push as far as Énoshima, but I doubt it. It will be our last day, as we shall sail the following morning for Kobe. As I run along the streets of Tokio in the afternoon, with the feeling that I have tried to set down, of things having narrowed as they become familiar, comes the excited melancholy of departure, and this same ugliness and prettiness have a new value as I look upon them for the last time. I sit in the little tea-house near the station, waiting for A——, and drink the "powdered tea," which tastes better than ever, as a stirrup-cup. And I do not resent the familiarity of a big Chinaman, proud of his English, and of national superiority here in size and commercial value, who addresses me and seeks to find out whether I, too, have a commercial value. My answers puzzle him, and he leaves me uncertain as to quantities, and walks off with the impudent majesty of his fellows among this smaller and less commercial race.

. . . At dinner I see at the table near me a Japanese gentleman, not very young, dining with his wife and another lady, who, I am told, is a well-known *gei-sha*. This information I receive from my more or less trusty courier, who also gives me some confused intimation that this gentleman had participated in the murder of Richardson, the Englishman, many years ago, under the old régime, for which murder somebody else was decapitated. The wife is correct and immovable, the *gei-sha* animated, with a great deal of color and charm. A German or Russian sits at another table, heavy, diplomatic, thick-bearded; the *gei-sha* recognizes him, rises, goes over to his table, and bends very low before him, almost kneeling; then speaks courteously and animatedly, as

161

if in compliment, to which the diplomat, without turning his head, says a word or two distantly. Then the *gei-sha* bends again down to the table, and walks respectfully backward, and then swings back into her seat. I am amused by this complete inversion of our own habits, and am reminded of the manners and assiduous attentions of our men at the theaters when they call on the indifferent fair. I see, too, that the points of attack and defense must be different.

The heat was still intense even in the night, within fifty yards of the sea; we went down to the quay and hired a boat with man and boy, to drift out into the hazy moonlight. The boy did the main part of the work: we lay in the boat, seeing nothing but this little body, and the flapping of its garments, and everything else a vague space of lightened shadow. We rowed or sculled far away, came near to a shore where there was a tea-house, for women opened its closed sides and, revealed by their lanterns, came down and called to us. But we pulled off, and later, in a far-off ocean with no shore nor sky, came across a little summer-house built on piles, through which the volume of the sea pressed and recoiled. Nothing could be more abandoned, more improbable. There was nothing in sight. Had we entered the little pavilion, and moored our boat or let it float away, we might have felt as if out in the distant sea. We were the center of a globe of pearl; no edges nor outlines of anything visible, except a faint circular light above, from which the pearly color flowed tremulously, and a few wrinkles of silver and dark below; no sound but a gentle sway of water. And we came home, having had the sense of the possibility of intense isolation in a fairyland of twilight.

AT SEA, OFF IZU, September 3.

We sailed this morning on the French steamer. It is now quite late in the afternoon. The Pacific keeps its blue under us, and a blue sea haze separates us from the violets and greens of the mountains of the shore, behind which the light is slowly sinking. All is gentle and soothing; but our captain says that he is not sure, and that *"hors d'Izu nous aurons la houle du Pacifique."* While waiting for this long, angry roll, I shall tell you about yesterday, of which there was little—for we had undertaken too much.

We left rather too late, and drove a good way in the foggy morning, passing much culture, and under many trees, of all of which I remember little. It was late when we stopped to breakfast at the little inn from which we were to be taken by *kuruma*, first to the big statue of Buddha, then wherever we might have time to go. We left the place, and reached the hollow between hills where the statue dwells, after passing through a curious deep cutting right through the rocks, which marks some old approach to the former city; for these hollows and fields were once covered by a great city, the city of Kamakura, the city of Yoritomo, and the great statue now out of doors was once in a temple of that city. Places are shown you in the dells: this was where was once the mansion of such a hero, here was that of the administrators of the military rule in the fifteenth century; here stood the palace where, with his two hundred and eighty last followers, such a one retired to perform harakiri, and perish in the flames, when overwhelming forces had captured the great city which was once the other capital of Japan. Trees and ordinary culture cover these spaces now.

And here was the temple. Sixty-three pillars supported its roof, and many of their bases are still there. But a great inundation from the sea, now some miles distant, destroyed the temple and its adjacent buildings. This happened as far back as the end of the fifteenth century, and the temple has not been rebuilt. The desire of Yoritomo to see the great statue made during his lifetime was not granted; but one of his waiting-ladies, after his death, collected the necessary funds, and it appears to have been cast in 1252 by Ono Go-rō-ye-mon. I know nothing about him, but if he be the artist, it is pleasant to record his name. The image is made of bronze cast in pieces brazed together and finished with the chisel. It is nearly fifty feet high as it sits; and if these points help you to its size, learn that its eyes, for instance, are four feet long, the length across its lap from knee to knee is thirty-five feet, and the circumference of the thumb is fully three feet. But these measures, though they show a large scale and great size, do not indicate a proportion, as we should understand it. The whole modeling is for effect, and the means and methods of the modeling are simple and elementary. Like all work done on archaic principles, the main accentuations are overstated, and saved in their relations by great subtleties in the large surfaces. It is emphatically modeled for a colossus; it is *not a little thing made big*, like our modern colossal statues; it *has always been big*, and would be so if reduced to life-size.

We saw it first from the side through trees, as we ran rapidly to the front, where are a temple gate, and a long courtyard still in order, that leads up to the statue. From the side one can see how it bends over, and rough as it is from behind, the impression of something real was strong as its gray form moved through the openings of the trees. The photographs must long have made you know it, and they also show the great base and the immense temple ornaments that stand upon it at the feet of the statue. They show also the little lodge at the side, where the priest in attendance lives, and gives information, and sells photographs and takes them, and generally acts as showman. We took many photographs from new points of view, and we even removed the thatch of a penthouse so as to get nearer and under the statue to the side; and I painted also, more to get the curious gray and violet tone of the bronze than to make a faithful drawing, for that seemed impossible in the approaching afternoon. We did not know how long a time we had spent lingering about it. The clouds had begun to open, and a faint autumnal light filled the little hollow, which has only small trees, and no imposing monuments like the great cryptomeria, which alone might seem fit to grow about here. All, on the contrary, was gentle and small—the lines of the hills, the trees, the garden plants about us: we might have been anywhere. Perhaps it is just as well; the whole impression comes from the statue, with the only objection or detraction that we can get near enough to it to see the mechanism, the means, and details of its expression. An accident, the breaking of its prison temple by a great cataclysm of nature, a great wave of the sea coming far inland and destroying the great building, has given to the statue something that it could never have had to the physical eye—in the degree it has now. Now, freed from its shrine, the figure sits in contemplation of entire nature, the whole open world that we feel about us, or its symbols—the land-scape, the hills, the trees and fields, the sky and its depths, the sunshine playing before the eyes of the seated figure, the air in which dance all the things that live in air, from the birds that fly to the atoms of dust, and the drifting leaves and blossoms, the confusion or the peace of the elements, the snow in crystals, and the rain drops. All this world of ours, which to the contemplative mind is but a figurative fragment of the universe, lies before the mental gaze of the Buddha. Unwinking, without change of direction, he looks forever; his will is forever subdued and held beneath him, as his fingers pressed together indicate his freedom from all the disturbances of that past of being which is subject to time and change, and his cognition, undisturbed, envelops and images the universe in final contemplation.

Astounding success of the artist in what he has really done, for there is no trace of means; the sum of realism is so slight, the conventional has so great a part; each detail is almost more of an ornament than of a representation. One almost believes that the result may be partly accidental: that, as one cannot fathom the reason of the expressiveness of a countenance, or of the influence of a few musical notes, even though one knows the mechanism, so it seems difficult to grant that there was once a choice in the other mind that caused it, that there were once many paths opened before it.

And still more do I believe that the accident of the great tempest has given a yet more patent and subtle meaning to the entire figure. Once upon a time its details, indeed, if not its entirety, must have looked more delicate in the reflected light of the temple building, when the upper part of the figure was bathed in mysterious gloomy light, while the lower glittered in answer to the openings of the doors. But could anything ever have rivaled the undecidedness of this background of veiled sky and shifting blue, which makes one believe at times that the figure soon must move? As one looks longer and longer at it, with everything around it gently changing, and the shadows shifting upon its surface, the tension of expectation rises to anxiety. The trees rustle and wave behind it, and the light dances up and down the green boughs with the wind; it must move—but there is no change, and it shall sit forever.

As we left, and I walked down the long pavement in front of the statue, in the early autumn sunshine and the rising freshness of the wind, I turned again and again, each time with the realization that the statue was still sitting, until we turned out of sight, a vague, unreasonable sense of having left it alone accompanying me, until other, different, light, and gay impressions broke the influence and allowed me to think of what I had seen as a work of art, such as I could understand and decompose—and, if I wished, make also.

And we lunched at Hase, near by, and from the comfortable inn could see on the gray hill above the temple of Kuwannon, and its red buildings and balustrades. After a very long lunch, we walked up to the temple, and from the platform in front looked toward the afternoon sea right before us, and the plain of Kamakura. Then we entered, and were taken in behind the great screen doors to a narrow but high place— lighted only from the little entrance—wherein stood right by us and over us a standing figure of the divinity, all golden in the dark. It is over thirty feet high, and whether it be great art or not,—for the darkness was too great to judge of form,—the glitter of a smile of gold far up above our heads, in the obscurity of the roof, was an impression that, even so near to the great statue out of doors, remains distinct. It was late afternoon; we dared look at no more statues, nor at relics of warriors of Kamakura, and started for the beach, partly with the hope of seeing Fuji behind us. But all was veiled in the sky; we walked along the beach, our *kurumas* dragging behind us, and crossed a little stream, and while A—— bathed in, and thereby took possession of, the Pacific, I walked up the sand-hills toward the little village at the end of the strand. As I came near it, an unfortunate distorted being, scarred with some leprous disease, plunged toward me in the twilight from some vague opening in the hills, and begged piteously, following me afterward with a thankful wail of "O Danna San! Danna San! Danna San!" that I hear yet. We reëntered our *kurumas* and drove in triumph to the inn of the little village. I say in triumph: *I* drove in triumph, observed of all observers—I had my usual costume and was clothed. A——, rather than wait to get dry, rode along with only a partial covering of *yukatta*, and attracted no attention. Had he had nothing on at all, he would have been still more in keeping with many of our neighbors. Night

167

was falling, nothing more could be done; we got back to our carriage and horses, and drove back in the warm darkness to Yokohama. And I close as we begin to feel the roll, "*la houle du Pacifique*."

KIOTO

September 16.

WE came into Kioto from Osaka, by rail, one fine afternoon. I had a half-childish hope of being surprised, a memory of days when, a boy, I read of the great forbidden city. Only a few years ago it was still forbidden, and now the little respectable car was hurrying us there as prosily as older life translates the verse of our early dreams. We were in September heat and glare. We passed over wide spaces of plain, edged by sharp mountains, looking hot and barren; through great plantations and stretches of green, with here and there a temple half hidden,—and over dried river-beds.

The station closed all views on our arrival, and the sudden transfer to streets showing no European influences was as if we had passed through a city's walls.

The first sensation was merely the usual one of a whirl through innumerable buildings, low, of wood, and more or less the same; extremely wide streets, all very clean; many people; a great bridge across the stony bed of a river almost dry; then some trees and little gardens and corners of temples with heavy roofs, as we turned through little roads and drove up to the gate of the hotel inclosure, which is placed on the edge of the outside hills and looks down upon Kioto. We were high up, in rooms looking over trees just below; next to us the corner of temple grounds that rounded away out of sight.

Early on most mornings I have sat out on our wide veranda

169

and drawn or painted from the great panorama before me—
the distant mountains making a great wall lighted up clearly,
with patches of burning yellow and white and green, against
the western sky. The city lies in fog, sometimes cool and
gray; sometimes golden and smoky. The tops of pagodas and
heavy roofs of temples lift out of this sea, and through it
shine innumerable little white spots of the plastered sides of
houses. Great avenues, which divide the city in parallel lines,
run off into haze; far away always shines the white wall of the
city castle; near us, trees and houses and temples drop out
occasionally from the great violet shadows cast by the
mountain behind us. Before the city wakes and the air clears,
the crows fly from near the temples toward us, as the great
bell of the temple sounds, and we hear the call of the gongs
and indefinite waves of prayers. Occasionally a hawk rests
uneasily on the thin branches below. Then the sun eats up
the shadows, and the vast view unites in a great space of
plain behind the monotony of the repeated forms of the small
houses, broken by the shoulders of the roofs and pagodas of
many temples. But near us are many trees and tea-houses
and gardens, and we are as if in the country.

We have worked conscientiously as mere sightseers until
all is confused as with an indigestion of information. I could
hardly tell you anything in a reasonable sequence, for in and
out of what I go to see runs a perpetual warp of looking at
curios, of which occupation I feel every day disgusted and
ashamed, and to which I return again as a gambler might,
with the hope of making it all right with my conscience by
some run of luck. This began on our very first day, when at
our first visit to an excellent merchant, for whom we had
letters, we spent the hours after dinner looking at the bric-à-
brac brought together for our purchase or amusement. We
had had the presentation and disappearance of the ladies of
the house after their customary genuflections; and a Euro-

pean dinner, waited upon, in part, by lesser clients of our entertainer. Meanwhile his one little girl sat beside him, half behind him, and occasionally betrayed her secret love for him by gently pressing his leg with the sole of her little stockinged foot. Japanese children are one of the charms of Japan, and this one is a type of their stillness; her sweet, patient face watching the talk of the elders, no change in her eyes revealing anything, but the whole person taking everything in—the little delicate person, which disappeared in a dress and sash not unlike her elders', except for color. Then there was a visit to another merchant, in the oldest house of the city, built low, so that none might perchance look down upon the sovereign lord's procession. Display of family relics—marriage gifts and complete *trousseaux* of the past; marriage dresses of the same time, symbolical in color,—white, red, and finally black. We are told to notice that the gold and silver fittings of precious lacquers are wanting, because many years ago some sumptuary edict of the Tokugawa government suddenly forbade the display or use of the precious metals in excess—a gradation to be determined by inspecting officials—for persons who, like merchants, should not pretend to pass a certain line.

Then, owing to other letters, we have paid our devoirs to the governor, and called, and subsequently received the polite attentions of his intelligent secretary. Under his guidance we visit the School of Art and see boys sketching, and enter rooms of drawing devoted respectively to the schools of the North and the South.

And we visit the school for girls, where the cooking-class is one bloom of peach-like complexions, like a great fruit-basket; where the ladylike teacher of gymnastics and child etiquette wears divided skirts; where the rooms for the study of Chinese classics and history contain a smaller number of fair students, looking more reasonable and much paler; and

171

where, on admiring in the empty painting-class a charming sketch of Kioto wharves, like the work of some lesser Rico, I am told that the fair artist has disappeared—married, just as if it had happened with us at home. But with a difference worth weighing gravely, for our guide and teacher informs me that the aim of this education is not to make girls independent, but rather to make more intelligent and useful daughters, sisters, or wives. And in this old-fashioned view I come to recognize the edges of a great truth.

Then temples, for Kioto is a city of temples; and every day some hours of hot morning have been given to visits, all of which make a great blur in my mind. The general memory is impressive and grand; the details run one into the other.

Thus we are paying dear for sightseeing, but it is impossible to set aside the vague curiosity which hates to leave another chance unturned. And when again shall I return, and see all these again? Now, however, all is associated with heat and glare, and with the monotony of innumerable repeated impressions, differing only in scale. Still, probably, when I shall have left I shall recall more clearly and separately the great solemn masses of unpainted wood, for which early forests have been spoiled; the great size of their timbers, the continuous felicity of their many roofings, the dreary or delicate solemnity of their dark interiors, the interminable recurrence of paintings by artists of the same schools; the dry and arid court-yards, looked at, in this heat of weather, from the golden shadows, where are hidden sometimes lovely old statues, sometimes stupid repetitions; images of the whole race of earlier shoguns; the harsh features of the great Taiko Sama, the sleek and subtle face of the great Iyéyasŭ, or the form of K'wan-on, carved by early art, leaning her cheek on long fingers; or noble, tapestried figures, rich in color and intensity of spotting, painted by the Buddhist Cho-Den-Su. . . .

I should like to describe the temple ceilings, in which are set the lacquered coffers of the war junk of Taiko, or of the state carriage of his wife. . . .

I have sketched in his reception hall, peopled to-day only by specters of the past—with gilt and painted panels on which may have looked the great Iyéyasŭ, who was to succeed him, and the blessed Xavier, and the early Jesuits, and the chivalric Christian lords who were to die on great battlefields. And close to a great room, where many monks bent over peaceful books, the little closet, with dainty shelves, in which Taiko looked at the heads of his dead enemies, brought there for inspection.

And we have gone up into the plain little pavilion, sacred to the ceremonies of tea-drinking, where the rough and shrewd adventurer offered to grim, ambitious warriors, as honorific guerdon for hard service, the simple little cups of glazed clay that collectors prize to-day.

I run over these associated details, because certainly the question of the great buildings is too weighty for my present mood. But the greater part of the romance of Japan is called up at every moment by what we see just now.

At Uji, among the tea gardens, we stopped on our way to Nara, the older capital, to see the temple of Bio-do-in and its "Phœnix hall," built in wood, that is now over eight hundred years old, its statues; its half-defaced paintings of the "Paradise in the West"; its high, dusty ceiling, inlaid with mother-of-pearl; and its sweet-toned bell.

And we saw the legendary bow of Yorimasa, which you will recall with me whenever you see a picture of the bow of the moon, across which flies the Japanese cuckoo. It was here that he defended Uji bridge, with a forlorn hope, against the army of the Taira, that his prince might have time to escape; and here, at Bio-do-in, while his last followers kept off the rush of the enemy, Yorimasa ran himself through with his sword, as a final duty paid to the honor of Japan.

On this side of the bridge, as I walked up other temple steps, hedged in by trees, with our friend Oye-San, the violet butterflies and blue dragon-flies crossed our path in every bar of sunshine.

At the monastery of Kurodani, on the edge of the mountain near us, are shown the graves of Nawozane and of the young Atsumori, whom he killed in battle. We are shown the portrait of the victim, painted in sorrow by the victor, and the pine-tree still stands upon which the warrior hung his armor when, tormented by remorse, he carried out his vow of never more bearing arms, and sought this place to enter religion and pray for the soul of the youth he had unwillingly slain. Strange flower of human pity, blooming out of the blood of civil wars like some story of Italy in the coeval day of St. Francis.

At that time the great war of the Genji and the Heike was devastating Japan, and in 1184, in a great battle by the sea, Yoshitsune, the hero of romance of Japan, serving his brother Yoritomo, whose story I told you at Nikko, defeated the Heike, and the "death of Atsumori" took place. This delicate boy, a prince of the Heike, scarcely sixteen years old, met in the battle the veteran Nawozane. Atsumori had fought bravely on the shore, having at first fled, and then returned, forcing his horse through the water. The greater strength of the older man prevailed, and the child fell under the blows of the powerful man-at-arms. When Nawozane disengaged his enemy's helmet, intending to take off the usual trophy of a head, the sight of the youthful face recalled his own son slain in battle, and he hesitated in inflicting on other parents a suffering like his own. But if he did not kill him others would, and his reputation would be endangered. He killed him, Atsumori bravely meeting death, and bore off the terrible trophy. Then, in the revulsion of remorse, he vowed himself to a religious life; he restored to Atsumori's father the son's fair head and his armor, and, going to Kioto, became a disciple in the religion of the holy Hónen Shónin, the founder of Kurodani; and there, near its lovely garden, are the tombs of the man and of the boy.

Or, while we are thinking of heads cut off, I pass again and again a lofty monument, under great trees, on a wide avenue beautifully macadamized, and kept in the trim of our Central Park, along which ride officers in Western uniform, or pass the police, in a dress whose type is borrowed from at least three European states. Under this tomb are buried the ears and noses of the Koreans slain in the wars that Hideyosni waged at the end of the sixteenth century. They were carried here as more convenient than the heads, the usual evidence of work well done, brought by the warriors to their commander. The memory of what the great pile means serves to confuse still more my admiration of the ultra-modern success of the wide carriage drive on which it stands.

OSAKA, September 18.

We have come to Osaka to spend an entire day in bric-à-brac: to arrive early at the big shop; to have tea offered us in the little back room of the merchant, which looks out and steps out upon his garden of a few trees and little pebbly walks and some stone lanterns—a garden that is for us, which his own may or may not be. Then cigars, and pieces of porcelain brought from the storehouses; then more tea, and an inspection of the many rooms full of odds and ends. Then more tea, and more pieces slowly and reluctantly drawn from the storehouse, as if we could not be so unreasonable; then lunch and tea, always in the house; then adjournment to the upper rooms, when the hundreds of kakemonos are unrolled, one after the other, to a crescendo of exasperation. Then

175

rediscussion of matters below-stairs and visits to other rooms full of wares not spoken of before; then more tea, and the last pieces grudgingly produced from the same occult store-houses; purchases amid final bewilderment; tea again, and departure.

We had come to Osaka on our way back from Nara, and we again return to Kioto, which we left three days ago. The trip to Nara was fatiguing and delightful, and I should like to recall it for you, but I have no time and have made no notes; and, besides, my memories are again beginning to merge one into another, and they themselves to blend with what I see in Kioto. But certainly something floats over, which a few lines can give.

We were out in our *kurumas* early in the morning, each with three runners. We found Oye-San waiting for us patiently, outside at Inari, where he had expected us from the earliest morning. It is from him that I get the little clay fox, given me for good luck, in a partnership with the one he retained. I need not speak of the heat. The roads were dusty and dry where they were not muddy and wet, in the country paths we took. We passed the edge of the city, which ends suddenly in rice fields, occupying what were once streets and houses. For Kioto is only a part of what it has been; and even when it was larger, not so many years back, it must still have been only the remainder of a greater past.

As we get into what is really the country, passing from broad road to narrow tracks, our runners sometimes lifted us over soft, wet places, or bumped us over narrow ditches, or guided us, at full tilt, on the edges of the stones that are bridges. Sometimes more patiently we halted to allow the files of black bulls to meander past us, dragging loads on wheels or carrying bales.

Rarely we met peasants, and then usually women, some-times with horses of a larger breed than that we saw last month in the east. Once, among rice fields in the basin of a circle of low hills, I saw the grove which covers the tomb of some divine emperor of early times. As we circled around the slope, far away from this solitary oasis of trees, we could see the grove on every side, finished and complete and rounded by time, as if sculptured in nature from some of those sketches that Japanese artists make for carving when they give all four sides, and the bottom, and the top, on a single page. Nothing else, but perhaps some uninscribed stone, marks the tomb of emperors, dotted about the plains of this oldest province of Japan. Strange enough, even in this strange country, is this evidence of the extreme simplicity in death, as in life, of the oldest line of Oriental despots, absolute lords and masters, ever-present patterns of the deity, who make this one solitary exception of simplicity in history. It is as if Japan itself was their tomb, as if they passed back into the nature of which their divine ancestors were gods—the gods of the sun and of the earth.

Blue hills and pagodas, and temples in the distance, and we came into Nara, which is but a breath, a ruin, a remnant of what it was. I had been told so often of the place, as a ruin among rice fields, that I was unprepared for the beautiful lay-out of what remains—for the well-planned roads and avenues, such as may well have belonged to some great capital, such as would have been heard of by travelers who, returning in days of Charlemagne from other Eastern cities to Byzantium, might have talked of Zipango.

Nothing remains but a few buildings, belonging to temples, but their approaches are splendid, even though there be often nothing more than the general grading and disposition. I should have written to you from our inn, where I looked, in the evening and morning, toward the slopes of distant hills, and heard, out of the darkness, the sound of the great bell which rang first some eleven centuries ago, and the

177

singing of the frogs in the fields which were once a city. It is now too late to begin to describe anything of what I saw; anything of temple buildings, from one of which to another we wandered, or of the old statues and relics, or of the religious dances of young girls which we looked at, standing or sitting near the balustrade of the dancing-shed, while inside, in the greater shade, they moved to the music and hymns of the priests—red and white figures, with long tresses of black hair and chaplets of flowers; with faces all painted white, and brilliant, indifferent eyes that saw me sketching clearly, however, and hands that waved, in a cadence of routine, fans and bunches of little bells with long streamers of violet, blue, green, red, and white. Or of the great park-like avenue, that made me think of England, through which still wander tame deer, as did those that, long ago, served as models for Okio the painters. I fear that what I have seen will remain only as an embroidery upon the stuff that my memory tries to unroll.

It was late on a sweltering afternoon when we managed to leave Nara, and we reached Horiuji for too short a visit; for we were due in Osaka the next day. We wandered in the late afternoon and evening through its courts, kindly received by the priests, for whom we had the recommendation of a friendly name.

At least I had time to see the Golden Hall, one of the earliest buildings, now more than twelve centuries and a half old, and the noble paintings on its walls attributed to some famous sculptor of that day. Their placid elegance, the refinement of their lines, their breath of religious peace, explained those claims to a solemn and glorious past for Japan, which look like a conventional exaggeration in a to-day that is delicate and small and dry.

The recall of Greek perfection was not forced, and while still vaguely unwilling to confuse one excellence by referring

178

to another, I could not help again thinking of the Greek and of Tanagra images, when I saw, by the light of the torches, in the great pagoda, as old as the great hall, groups modeled in clay by the same old sculptor, whose name is given to the paintings—Amida, and Kuwan-on, and Monju, and the scenes of the death of Buddha. An admirable antiquity was to be the continuous impression of the evening, carried out into our last looks at the Treasure House. Its very air of an old New England barn or crib raised upon posts, its rough red painting, the high wooden steps of entrance, the gigantic wooden latch-key with which the guardian priest fumbled at its door, gave the note of extreme early simplicity—the feeling of a persisting indifference to the adornments and changes of centuries of fashions.

It has been useless all along to detail anything, but the impressions of the last things seen remain with me as types of all. For there hung on the old walls of the Treasure House a framed banner, once carried in ancient battles, its brocaded pattern exactly like that which we know in Babylonian art: the circles with the lilies between, and in each circle the Assyrian monarch struggling with lions—imitation or original of coeval Sassanian Persia, I suppose, but housed here all these thousand years, and in its persistence of pattern connecting with that heavy and oppressive antiquity of Nineveh which knows nothing older than itself for our story, except oldest Egypt.

But I was yet to find something old that would be directly meant for me,—a painting by the legendary painter of Japan, the Cimabue of a thousand years ago, inheritor or student of still older Chinese art—Kose-no-Kanaoka.

The painting is still in fair condition, though injuries of time reveal, as usual, the methods used by the painter. And it was a delight in me, in this mood of veneration for past greatness, to recognize in the veilings and sequences of this painting of the lotus methods I had used myself, working at such distance of time and place, when I had tried to render the tones and the transparency of our fairy water-lily; and I know you will forgive the superstitious sense of approval of my re-inventions from this indefinite past of art.

We wandered among the buildings until night had set in; we signed on the register of visitors, and contributed a small sum to the repairs of these decaying relics of the greatness of Japan; we received some little gifts of impressions and prints in acknowledgment, and then rested in the neighboring inn, waited upon by fat, good-natured tea-girls, most certainly belonging to to-day.

We had now to take a long night ride, and at length we rushed out into the moonlight, our fourteen runners appearing and disappearing as we came in and out of the shadows in the long procession of our train.

We whirled past the houses of the small town, indiscreetly close to the paper screens, lighted from within, against which were profiled the shadows of faces, sometimes with pipes or cups lifted to their lips or the outlines of coiffures piled up on the head — all pictures more Japanese than their very originals; then between rounded hills on which stood masses of maple-trees; then near to empty spaces of water; then sank into dark hollows, at the bottom of which rivers ran as fast the other way.

I watched and looked as long as fatigue allowed, but fell asleep in the uncomfortable kuruma, waked every now and then by some sudden jolt to my extended arm and head.

Occasionally I had dreamy glances at what I remember as a vast plain, with lofty, colorless mountains at one side, and perhaps I saw glimpses of the sea. The night air was cool in the hollows after the sweltering day, and I found my arm and face damp with the dew. A Japanese poet would have said that it was but the spray from off the oars of some heavenly boat which sailed that night across the starry stream of the Milky Way.

In the dawn we saw the white walls of the castle of the city of Osaka, and ran across its many bridges, all silent in the morning.

September 19.

We spent the late afternoon and early evening in the state apartments of the temple of the Green Lotus, where we looked at strange dances and listened to curious music.

All was sacred and mystic, according to traditions transmitted orally from early ages, and all the more liable to disappear as the heredity of occupation which has been the mark of Japan is more more and more endangered by modern views and modern "openings."

When we had wandered through those shady apartments in the long, low buildings of the temple gardens, and had seen the paintings of their screen walls, and the carvings of their transoms, we sat down in one of the largest rooms, the wall screen was removed which divided us from another, and we had then a ready-made stage before us. Light came in from the open veranda, now stripped of all screens, against whose platform many unbidden, unofficial guests, acquaintances of acquaintances, and people about the temple, leaned in a mass of heads and arms and busts. Outside the light was filtered green and orange through the trees, and caught the edges of all forms in the shade within. The orchestra of flutes and drums occupied a little recess, from behind which the dancers appeared in turn. Behind the musicians, a great violet curtain, with three temple crests in white, made a twilight background for their white and blue dresses, gilded by the lights in the tall candlesticks on the floors before them. With the sound of the instruments two boys came around the corner of the screen, and, saluting, stepped off in short, zigzag movements, evidently learned by rote, and which had a certain strange elegance. They were performing the butterfly dance, and made out very distinctly the crisscross flight of the insects. When they lighted or poised before lighting their feet struck the ground and they swayed without stepping away. They wore butterfly wings, and wide sleeves melting into them, and their silver diadems, filled up with twigs of flowering plants, made out a faint fringe of antennæ. They wore the ugly ancient trousers of yellow silk, and long trains of embroidered green satin trailed on the mats behind them. Broad bands of blue and white across the chest, and a white belt, recalled the insect original, and blue and white wings drooped over their wide green satin garments. Each carried a flowering branch in his hand. It was all more strange than beautiful, with a mysterious impression of remote antiquity, as if invented for some prehistoric Polynesian worship. In some of the next dances, whose names I do not remember, and which were carried out by men, the flat mask, with a wide triangle for eyes and another for the mouth, made out just this similitude. In another dance two men glided about the room, listening and finding their way; then warriors in antique Chinese costume, with great helmets and halberds, and coats of mail, and long trains, appeared singly and by twos, and marched and counter-marched; and finally, standing by their lances, laid at their feet, drew and held up their swords, while each other peaceful hand was extended in the gesture that we know as the pontifical blessing; and this ended the dance of "Great Peace," probably some relic of early triumphant Chinese dynasties.

It was now evening: the blue light of the open veranda made large square openings in the golden room. Outside, against the balustrade, pressed dark forms, with faces reddened by the light inside—the outside lookers-on. Inside, the gold walls and the gilded ceiling, the great gold temple drum, the yellow mats, and the white dresses of the musicians, made a soft bloom like the hollow of a lotus, when the last performer, in rose-red and crimson, glided into the room, swinging from side to side, and brandishing a gilded scepter. Uncouth gestures and enormous strides, with no meaning that I could make out, a frightful mask that hung far away from the face, with loose jaw and projecting mane and a long red, pointed hood, made an impression as barbarous, as meaningless, as splendid, and as annoying as what we might feel before the painted and gilded idol of some little known and cruel creed. This was the dance of "*Ra* Dragon King," and closed the entertainment.

We exchanged some words with the late performers in their insignificant everyday clothes, and rode home in the twilight through the little roads, where Kioto gentlemen were rushing their horses up and down, wrapped in wide riding trousers, which fluttered along the horses' flanks. . . .

We have also given a *soirée.* — that is to say, a supper, with the proper trimmings of musical entertainment and dancing, and were probably the most amused of all the people there. The amusement consisted, in great measure, of our not knowing just what we were going to have, for otherwise the details were simple to monotony. We had one of the upper floors of a fashionable inn. It was very hot, and we were glad to find that we should be at supper in our loosest bath robes. There was nothing unusual—though everything is novel to us—but the extreme smallness of the many *gei-shas*, who sat between us at the end of the dinner, passed the *sakè*, said witty things, of which we understood not one word, gave us much music on the *samisen* (the three-stringed guitar) and on the flute, and sang, and gave us dances. But they were absolutely incredible in the way of littleness. It did not seem possible that there were real bones inside their narrow little wrists and dolls' fingers. What there was in most of their little heads I don't know, but I could have imagined sawdust. For the doll illusion, for the painted face and neck and lips, all done upon the same pattern from pure conventionality (not at all like our suggestive painting), and the sudden stopping sharply at a line on the little slender neck, gave me the feeling of their having artificial heads. The gentle little bodies disappeared entirely inside of the folds of the dress and the enormous bows of the sash. And when the tall youngsters, Americans, whom we had invited, began to romp with the playthings, late in the evening, I felt anxious about possible breakage, such as I remember, in nursery days, when we boys laid hold of our sisters' dolls.

But this artificial impression disappears as with all novelty in people, and when one of the youngest of these child-women, at some moment in the evening, removed the mask of the jolly fat woman (that you know by the prints), behind which she had been singing, the little sad face told its contradictory story as touchingly as with any of her Aryan sisters. And late in the evening, when the fun, I suppose, was uproarious, we went to the extreme of writing and painting on fans, and one of our merchant guests wasted India-ink in mock tattooing of his bared arm and shoulder.

September 21.

We leave to-morrow morning.

This has been Sunday, our last day in Kioto. I have been trundled all day in a fearful rain, to see last sights, to look up shops for the last time. My runners have taken me to this or that place, near the great temples, where I hope finally to decide upon some little Buddha or Amida, which have tempted me among other sculptures, and I have dallied in the other shops that supply the small things that adhere to worship, and finally I have made a long visit to the good lady who has sold me pottery, and who once shocked my Western prudery by dilating upon the merits of unmentionable designs and indescribable bric-à-brac.

At length I return in the gray noon, giving a last look at each shop that I know; at the long façade of the "Inn of Great Wealth," at the signs and the flags of the theater; at the little *gei-shas* trotting about in couples, whom I recognize (for how can I tell them from those whom I know?); at the quaint, amusing little children, always a fresh delight; at the little pavilion near us, where the archers shoot; at the places where horses stand under the trees to be ridden by amateurs; at the small tea garden's pretty gates; at the latticed windows which open in the dusk; and then, with their coats sticking to their backs, and wet, stained legs, my runners leave me at the gate of the hotel; final settlement of purchases in boxes, packing, and receiving visits of departure.

In the late afternoon we go to the temples on the edge of the hill near us (the temples of Kiyomidzu) with two of our good friends and their children. Our runners insist upon dragging and bumping us up many steps, and finally escort us, almost to the temple itself, in a procession of double file, which, like a long tail, halts when we stop, and again waggles after us in uncertainty when we set off anew. We walk along the ascending street and stop to bargain at the innumerable little shops, full of little odds and ends, half playthings and half religious emblems or images, which are sold certainly to the pleasure of the many children who throng the place. And I, too, feel pleased at having children with us, and at having occasionally the timid little fingers of Miss Kimi in mine. In her other small hand she holds a fan that I painted yesterday for her father, and I wonder occasionally whether she wishes me to notice her possession. I surmise that the foreign gentleman gives her sometimes a little doubtful fear, as I catch her eyes looking up cautiously from below her "bangs." We talk, exactly of what it would be hard to say, for there is not with us enough of any one language "to go round," and our interpreter has been left out; but we feel distinctly that we understand each other, and our older companions explain quite a number of things in this partnership of a few words.

We ascend the high steps on one side of the tower and pass with the Sunday crowd through the great hall, like a corridor, along which are seated on altar steps golden images of gods, in a shadow dusted by the long beams of the afternoon sun, that pour across it from one open side. Through this veil of dancing motes we see the statues and the great gilded lotuses and candelabra, and the forms of attendant priests, and the crowd that passes, and that stops for a moment in prayer. The words that they repeat come into cadence with the shuffling of their feet, and the creaking of the planks of the flooring, and the sounds of the dropping of offerings.

The crowd is quiet, orderly, but amused at being out. The women smile out of their slanting eyes and walk leaning forwards, and their black hair shines like lacquer, and the artificial flowers in the great folds of the coiffure dance in the sunlight. They are quietly dressed, all but the young girls, who wear bright colors and blue satin sashes. The men slide about, also in quiet silk or cotton. A large part of them are dressed in every shade of blue; occasionally the bare leg comes out, but all wear holiday dress, except our runners or their fellows, who keep their workday looks. And the children—they are all everywhere, and all at home; they are all dressed up, with full, many-colored skirts, and showy sashes, and every little head with some new and unexplainable spot of tonsure.

Many of the crowd turn around the building, or its veranda, touching the columns with their hands and following tracks, worn deep like ruts, in the planking of enormous

186

thickness. Oye-San points this out to me, and indicates its religious intention. Both he and our other companion clap their hands and pray for a moment. A wave of seriousness and abstraction passes over their faces; then again all is as before, and we step out upon the wide balcony, which, built upon gigantic piles, hangs over a deep hollow filled with trees and buildings, all in the shadow now. From below rise, with the coolness of the green trees and grass, the sounds of dropping waters. In time we descend the path and the steps, and drink from one of the streams which fall from gigantic gargoyles, out of a great mass of wall.

But it is late: we look again upon Kioto from the temple above, all swimming in light and haze, and walk back to our *kurumas*; a final good-by to the children, but we shall see their parents again; and then we return, and look from our veranda for the last time at the city stretched out in the evening, lost almost entirely in the twilight of a great lake of violet fog. A few shapes are just felt in the misty space, but no more than as waves in water, or as greater densities in the undulations of the colored vapor. So uncertain is everything that the nearest temple building loses its place, and floats all below its roof; but its wet tiles glitter, reflecting the rose-colored drift in the highest pale turquoise sky.

Below us, the trees make a delicate pattern of dark wet lace.

Then the rose-color deepens and dulls, the upper sky becomes colorless; all floats in unreal space, and Kioto dis-appears from before my eyes: forever, I suppose—as the charm of this scene, which will never come again; as the little maiden whom I met to-day, only for an eternal good-by.

A JAPANESE DAY—FROM KIOTO TO GIFU

NAGOYA. September.

NOTWITHSTANDING the long parting, which kept us up very late, the same courteous Japanese friends were at the hotel in the morning to bid us a still more final good-by. Oye-San alone remained faithful to his self-intrusted care of us, and determined to see us as far as the land would allow,—that is to say, to the shores of Biwa Lake.

The caravan was smaller now, diminished by our parting with Awoki, the interpreter, and the men necessary to trundle him about. Still we were a goodly company,—nineteen men in all, of whom two were masters, one the servant, and the rest the runners who were to get us and our baggage to Otzu on Biwa Lake long before noon. There was to be no novelty on our road, it being merely the highway from the capital to the lake. It was a lovely morning, the sun long risen, and all the places and buildings now a part of our memories glistening in the shadow and the dew. We turned our backs for the last time on Kiyomidzu, and ran through the great gate of the temple near us; then, bumping down the steep steps under it, skirted the great wall of Dai Butzu and the interminable side of the Sanjiu sangendo (the hall of the thirty-three spaces),[1] along which in old times the archers used to shoot. Then we gradually got out of the city, into the road filled with traffic going both ways. There seemed to be no break between town and country. Here and there the mountain side, covered with trees, descended to the road.

[1] Three hundred and eighty-nine feet long.

But the effect was that of a long street, deep among hills, and continuously spotted with buildings. Long trains of beautiful black bulls, drawing lumber or merchandise, or carrying straw-covered bales, streamed peacefully along. We passed peasant women,—hardy, tall, sometimes handsome, with scarlet undergowns held up; occasionally one riding on a pack-horse, or in her place a child perched on the hump of the wooden saddle. Or, again, peasants bearing loads on their backs, or carriers with weighty merchandise swung between them on poles; priests, young and old, stepping gravely in their white, or yellow, or black dresses—some with umbrellas open, others, whose quicker step meant that they had not far to go (perhaps only to some wayside temple), protecting their shaven heads with outspread fan. Or a kuruma, usually with one runner, taking into town, economically, two women together, one old, one young, and followed by another kuruma carrying some old gentleman, very thin or very fat, the head of a family. Kurumas carrying Japanese tourists or travelers, with hideous billycock hats, or Anglo-Indian helmets, or wide straw hats *à la mode de* Third Avenue, these abominable head-pieces contrasting with their graceful gowns, as did their luggage, wrapped up in silk handkerchiefs with their European traveling rugs. Or, again, other kurumas carrying unprotected females in pairs, with the usual indifferent or forlorn look; or couples of young girls more gaily dressed, with flowery hairpins, the one evidently a chaperon to the other; then a Government official, *all* European, with hurrying runners; sometimes, but rarely, the Japanese litter, or *kago*, or several if for a party, their occupants lying at their ease as to their backs, but twisted into knots as to their feet, and swaying with the movement of the trotting carriers. Bent to one side by the heavy ridgepole, which passes too low to allow the head to lie in the axis of the body, sweet-eyed women's faces, tea-rose or peach-colored, looked up from the bamboo basket of the litter. With proper indifference their lords and masters looked at us obliquely. On the roofs was spread a miscellaneous quantity of luggage.

From time to time troopers or officers, of course in European costume, mounted on Japanese chargers, cantered past. Two hours of this; then the sides of the road, which had risen and fallen with hill and valley, melted away, and the harbor of Otzu and Lake Biwa and blue mountains over the water, and others sketched in the air, were spread before us in the blaze of sunlight seen through the cool shadow of the mountains.

We rode down the hill to a little jetty, marvelously like a North River dock, with big sheds where passengers were waiting, and a little steamer fastened to the wharf. We bade good-by for the last time to Oye-San, who said many things that we appreciated but did not understand the words of, and who pointed to the square Japanese sails glittering in the far-off light, saying, "Fune, Fune!" ("The boats, the boats!") We dismissed kurumas and kurumaya and sailed off with Hakodate (the courier) alone. We stretched ourselves on the upper deck, half in sun, half in shadow, and blinked lazily at the distant blue mountains and the great sea-like lake.

Two hours later we had landed at a long jetty, in a heavy sea, with tossing dark blue water, different from the quiet azure of our sail. The brisk wind, blowing the white clouds over the blue sky, was clear and cold. We get out of its reach, as I felt neuralgic, and tried to sleep in a little tea-house, waking to the screams of the tea-house girl, "Mairimasho!" and I had but time to get into the train. Whether it started from there or had arrived there, I never knew. I had been glad to forget everything in dreamland.

I remember little of my railroad ride, what with neuralgia and heat, and the effects of the dance of the little steamer on Lake Biwa. There were mountains and ravines, and vast

190

engineering protections for our path, and everywhere the evidence of a struggle with the many running waters we crossed or skirted. The blue and silver of the lake that we had crossed, and the sweetness of its air, were shut out in the dust and the heat of mountain sides. We had not seen the Eight Beauties of Biwa Lake.[1] The "Autumn Moon from Ishiyama" had set long before we passed, and the idea of other temples to be seen brought out A——'s antagonism to more climbing, only to be rewarded by promenades through lanterns and shrines and confused struggling with dates and divinities. "The Evening Snow on Hira-yama" was not to fall until we should be across the Pacific; nor could we ask of that blue September morning "The Blaze of Evening at Seta" nor "The Evening Bell of Mii-dera"—though we heard the bell early, and wondered whether it were still uninjured, from the time when big Benkei carried it off and exchanged it for too much soup, exactly seven hundred years ago; nor "Rain by Night at Karasaki," the place of the famous pine-tree, which was growing, they say, twenty-four hundred years ago, when Jimmu was emperor. There I might have met, perhaps, the "Old Man and the Old Woman" you have seen over and over again in the pictures and on the fans. (They are the spirits of the other old pine-trees of Takasago and Sumiyoshi, and they are fond of visiting each other.) Nor did we see "The Wild Geese alighting at Katada," but I felt as if I had seen "The Boats sailing back from Yabase" and "The Brigh Sky with a Breeze at Awadzu." If I had not, I still had seen boats sailing over and under as lovely a blue as can be spread by early September days. I suppose that our friend Oye-San was trying to recall these last classical quotations to me when he bade me good-by at the landing in Otzu. An ocean rolls between his Parnassus and ours, but he lives much nearer to the mood that once made beautiful the names of

[1] Omi-no-hakkei.

Tempe and Helicon and the winding Meander.

With all this dreaming I fell asleep, and woke free from pain, but stupid and unimpressionable, as our train stopped at the little station from which we were to ride to Gifu. This was a little, new way-station (of course I don't remember its name), so like, and so unlike, one of ours, with the same look of the railroad being laid down—"imposed"—on an earth which did not understand what it all meant—grass struggling to get back to the sides of filled-up ditches; timbers lying about; new, astonished buildings, in one of which we washed, and waited, and dined. Meanwhile Hakodate went after the runners who were to drag us on our afternoon ride, and then, if "we suited," to run with us the whole week, thirty-five miles a day, along the Tokaido, back toward Yokohama.

When all was ready it was late afternoon, and our procession ran along what seemed to be a vast plain of table-land, with high mountains for an edge. All seemed as clear and neat as the air we rode in. Somewhere there we must have passed the hill of "The Turning Back of the Chariot": this means that, long ago,—that is to say, about 1470,—the regent Yoshimoto, while traveling here, found that the inhabitants, to do him honor, had put in order, neat and trim, the thatch of every building. What the prince was looking for is what we call the picturesque. To miss all the charms that ruin brings was too much for his esthetic soul, and he ordered the wheels of his chariot to be turned for home. So did not we. Neater and neater grew the inclosures, farms, and villages; the fences had pretty gates,—curious patterns of bamboo pickets,—a far-away, out-of-the-world flavor of Holland or Flanders. Even the ordinary setting out of wayside trees, in this province of forestry, insisted on the analogy, confused perhaps with a dream of Lombard plains and mountains in a cool blue distance, for the mind insists on clinging to reminiscences, as if afraid to trust itself to the full sea of new impressions.

As I rode along, so neat and clean was each picture, framed in sunlight if we were in shadow, or in clear shade when we were in sunlight, that I thought I could remember enough small facts for sketches and notes when I should get to Gifu. We reached Gifu in the early twilight, and had no special one impression; we were framed in by the streets, and confused by turning corners, and disturbed by anxiety to get in. But we had one great triumph. Our guide was new to the place— as we were; and we chose our inn at our own sweet will, with a feeling of authority and personal responsibility delicious to experience after such ignominy of guidance. Up we went to our rooms, and opening the *shojis* [1] looked out upon the river, which seemed broad as a great lake. Our house was right upon it, and the open casement framed nothing but water and pointed mountains, stealing away in the obscure clearness of a colorless twilight. The running of the river, sloping down from the hills on a bed of pebbles, cut off the noises of the town, if there were any, and the silence was like that of far-away country heights. In this semi-painful tension the day's pictures disappeared from my mind. I was all prepared to have something happen, for which I should have been listening, when suddenly our host appeared, to say that the boats were coming down the river. The chilly evening air gave us new freshness, and off we started, deaf to the re-monstrances of Hakodate, who had prepared and set out his very best for supper. We rushed past the artist in cookery, whose feelings I could yet appreciate, and plunged after our host into the dark streets. In a few minutes we were by the riverside, and could see far off what we took for our boat, with its roof and lanterns. The proffered backs of our lantern-bearing attendants gave the solution of how we were to get to

[1] Sliding screens, which take the place of our windows.

it. Straddling our human nags, we were carried far out into the shallow, pebbly river, landed into the boat, and poled out into deeper water, nothing to be seen but the night and the conical hills, one of which I fancied to be Inaba, where was once Nobunaga's castle. Some faint mists were white in the distance, as if lighted by a rising moon. At no great distance from us, perhaps at a quarter of a mile, a light flickered over the water. On our approach we could distinguish a man connected with it, who apparently walked on the dark surface. He was evidently a fisherman or a shrimper, and his movements had all the strangeness of some long-legged aquatic bird. He knew his path, and, far out, followed some track or ford, adding to the loneliness as does a crane in a marshy landscape. Then I saw him no more, for he headed up the river toward an opening between the hills. Suddenly a haze of light rounded the corner of the nearest mountain, then grew into a line of fire coming toward us. Above the rustle of the river's course, and our own against it, came the beating of a cry in unison. The line of flame broke into many fires, and we could see the boats rushing down upon us. As quickly as I can write it, they came in an even line, wide apart—perhaps fifty feet or so—enough for us to pass between, whereupon we reversed our movement and drifted along with them. In the front of each boat, hung upon a bent pole, blazed a large cresset filled with pine knots, making above a cloud of smoke, starred with sparks and long needles of red cinders. Below, in the circle of each light, and on its outer rim, swam many birds, glossy black and white cormorants, straining so at the cords that held them that they appeared to be dragging the boats. As they spread like a fan before the dark shadow of the bows, the cords which fastened them glistened or were black in the night. Each string ran through the fingers of the master-fisher at the bows, and was fastened to his waist and lost in the glittering straw of his rain-skirt. Like a four-in-hand driver, he seemed to feel his birds' movements. His fingers loosened or tightened, or, as suddenly, with a clutch pulled back. Then came a rebellious fluttering, and the white glitter of fish in the beaks disappeared—unavailingly; each bird was forcibly drawn up to the gunwale, and seized by the neck encircled by its string-bearing collar. Then a squeeze—a white fish glittered out again and was thrown back into the boat. The bird scuttled away, dropped back into the water, and, shaking itself, was at work again. They swam with necks erect, their eyes apparently looking over everything, and so indifferent to small matters as to allow the big cinders to lie unnoticed on their oily, flat heads. But, every few seconds, one would stoop down, then throw back its head wildly with a fish crosswise in its mouth. When that fish was a small one it was allowed by the master of the bird to remain in the capacious gullet. Each pack guided by a master varied in numbers, but I counted thirteen fastened to the waist of the fisherman nearest to us. Behind him stood another poling: then farther back an apprentice, with a single bird, was learning to manage his feathered tools. In the stern stood the steersman, using a long pole. Every man shouted, as huntsmen encouraging a pack, "Hoo! Hoo! Hoo!"—making the cry whose rhythm we had heard when the flotilla bore down upon us.

Ten minutes, a quarter of an hour, more passed as we kept alongside with motionless celerity. I tried to sketch in the insufficient light—making sometimes one sketch right upon another, so little could I see my lines in the treacherous light. Then the boats swerved off and were driven to the shore together, or as far as we could get to it, in the shallow water. Above us rose the steep green hillside, the trees and rocks lit up in an arabesque of light and dark by the now diminished flames.

The birds rested, standing in the water, preening their oily backs and white bellies, and flapping their ragged wings, which seemed to have been clipped. The apprentice caressed his bird, the fishermen and the steerers laughed and exchanged jokes and chatted generally, with all the good nature and making light of hard work which is so essentially Japanese.

Then the birds began to fight, and to show that peace was not their pleasure. Fresh pine knots were thrown into the cressets; each man took his place; the polers pushed off; the birds strained at the strings; and all *da capo*. A little longer we watched, and then we let the boats glide past us; the fires faded again into a haze of light as they went down the river toward the bridges of the town, now dotted with people.

Then we were carried to the shore as we had left it, and were piloted home through the streets, now filled with lanterns and movement. We found our outraged artist in cookery still indignant over our neglect of food, but he was gradually appeased, and made up for his hungry masters a fairly sufficient meal. Cigars, a scrutiny of my despairing sketches, and a long look at the lovely melancholy of the river and mountains before we closed the *shojis* for the night.

FROM KAMBARA TO MIYANOSHITA—A
LETTER FROM A KAGO

September 28.

I AM writing in a *kago*.[1] You do not know what an achievement this is, but I shall explain later on what a kago is, why I am in it, and why it is not exactly the place to expect a letter from. To begin at the beginning, we were yesterday afternoon at Kambara, on the gulf of Suruga Bay. We had eaten there in an inn by the water, while I watched through the screens the waving of a palm tree in the wind, which was now blowing autumnally and had cleared the sky and enlivened us with a hope of continuous view of Fuji. Along the beach, as we rode away, the breakers ran far up the sand, and the water was green as emerald from the brown, wet shore to the distant blue haze of the ocean in the south. At the end of the great curve of the gulf stretched the lines of green and purple mountains, which run far off into Idzu, and above them stood Fuji in the sky, very pale and clear, with one enormous band of cloud half-way up its long slope, and melting into infinite distance toward the ocean. Its nearest point hung half across the mountain's base, more solid than the mountain itself, and cast a long shadow upon it for miles of distance. Above, the eye could but just detect a faint haze in the delicate blue of the sky. Best of all weather, we thought; a breeder of bad weather, according to our men, who, alas! knew more of it than we did. For a mile now, perhaps, we ran along between the sea and the abrupt green wall of hills, so steep that we could not see them, and, turning sharply

[1] You may pronounce kang'go.

197

around a corner, beheld Fuji, now filling the entire field of sight, seeming to rise even from below us into the upper sky, and framed at its base by near green mountains; these opened as a gate, and showed the glittering streak of the swollen Fujikawa, the swiftest river in Japan.

The lower eastern slope was cut off by clouds, but its western line, ineffably delicate in clearness, stretched to the left out of our range of vision. Below its violet edge the golden slope spread in the sun, of the color of an autumn leaf. Along the center of this province of space the shadow of the great cloud rested. The marks of the spurs of the mountain were as faint as the streaks of the wind on a grain-field. Its cone was of a deep violet color, and as free of snow as though this had been the day of poetic tradition upon which the snow entirely disappears to fall again the following night. No words can recall adequately the simple splendor of the divine mountain. As A—— remarked, it was worth coming to far Japan for this single day.

Right into this marvelous picture we rode, through green plantations and rice-fields, which edged the bases of the nearest hills and lay between us and the river. There we found no means of crossing. All bridges had been carried away by the flood. The plain was inundated; travelers had been detained for a week by a sea of waters, and were scattered there and in neighboring villages, filling every resting-place; and, worst of all, the police officials would not allow us to tempt the fishermen to make the dangerous crossing.

The occasion was a solemn one. The police representative, upon seeing us come in person to request help, slipped off the easy Japanese dress which he was wearing in these days of forced idleness, and reappeared from behind the screen clad in his official European costume. I have no doubt that our interpreter explained to him what important persons we were, and what important letters we bore to important people

of the land, for he kindly suggested that we might sail past
the mouth of the river, from near Kambara, whence we had
just come, so as to land far away from the spread of all this
devastation; and he offered to send a deputy with a requisition
for a junk and sufficient sailors from the nearest fishing-
village on the bay—and so we returned. While Hakodate
and the messenger went on to make all arrangements, A——
and myself stopped at the place where we had had our view
of Fuji, to make a more careful sketch. You can have no idea
of how much closer the clearer mind worked out the true
outline of the mountain, which my excitement had height-
ened at least a couple of thousand feet; nor should I forget
how my two-legged horse of a runner held my paint-box for
me, and seemed to know exactly when and where I wished to
dip my brush. It seemed to me that only a few moments had
passed when the messenger returned to say that the boat was
ready to launch, and that we must hurry to be out at sea
before sunset; this too in view of the storm, which we might
escape if we hurried. The implied threat made no impression
on me. The picture before us had not changed any more than
if painted by man. The great cloud hung fixed, apparently,
in the same place. All was still: perhaps in the uppermost sky
one would distinguish some outlines of white in the blue.
Still we hurried off, and arrived upon a scene of confusion
and wild excitement. A captain and a crew had been found;
their boat stood high up on the crest of the surf, now beating
on the shore, and carried the line with which to pull out the
small junk, still far up on the beach. The wheels of our
kurumas had been taken off and their bodies had been placed
in the hold.

As we got on board at least a hundred naked men pushed
and tugged to start the junk upon the slope of sand. The sun
was setting suddenly behind the headland of Shizuoka, and
the air was filled with the moisture from the sea; a rosy

bloom, pink as the clouds themselves, filled the entire air, near and far, toward the light. On the other side the distance was fading into gray and violet mist. The great mountain was still a great clear mass, but colorless, like the northern sky behind it, while, bathed in the color of fairyland, we rose and fell over the breakers — the spray, the waves, the boat, the bodies of the men, glistening and suffused with pink.

No painter ever saw a more ideal light. And suddenly it faded, leaving us in a still brilliant twilight, through which we looked at the tossing of the hazy sea. The mast was lifted and set, the great square sail was hoisted, and the captain took hold of the ponderous tiller. We stretched ourselves on the poop deck, prepared for a dance of seventeen miles; then under my protecting blanket I fell asleep — to wake and see before me a sheet of rain. The predicted storm had flooded us; we lay in the water that covered the deck, our waterproofs insufficient, and glad to be able to find some protection under the Japanese rain-coats of straw, whose merits I had not yet understood.

From under my shelter I could see that our mast was lowered, and that the captain and the sailors forward were working at the heavy sweeps. Below, under hatches, I could hear the groaning of our seasick runners. Between the gusts of rain came the voice of the captain, now in the straining agony of seasickness, next keeping up a steady, chanted talk with a mate forward. A lantern was lashed to the post of the tiller, and the captain's bare feet rose and fell with his steps at the great oar, showing sharply the action of tendons and muscles. I tried to sketch under my cover, then dozed, — sleepy with the rocking and the cold and the wet, — and with every waking hearing the whistling of the wind and the continuous monotonous voice in a language not understood. So passed the night.

We saw the morning break on a lonely, high, gray bank,

streaked by the sea lines of different tides, and crowned with a line of pines of all sizes and shapes, stretching for miles dark green against the white clouds which covered the base of the mountains behind. Out of these white banks stood dull blue peaks, while the highest mountains were lost in cloud, and all was gray and desolate with the rain. The surf broke on the sand not more than a hundred yards from us. We lay there some time, waiting for more light, for all wind had ceased; then four men swam ashore with a rope, and towed us along the bank. The surf had abated, but landing was too difficult, and we were to be dragged, while our other men worked at the big sculls and pushed us along. We wore along four miles to a little bar, over which we were pulled by the men now in the water into a singular little harbor with an entrance not more than a hundred feet wide. On this the surf broke gently—white on the gray sea. To our left the backs of two sand-spits dotted the water, and on the right, looking out to sea, rose the edge of a grove of pines, with four or five houses, heavy roofed and thatched, against its green darkness.

On the curve of the beach before it stood a high pointed rock almost touched by the water, edged around and covered with pines—all but the perpendicular side facing the harbor. On its summit stood a little red temple, whose back we saw. On the other side, landwards, as we left our boat and followed our guides ashore around its base, a hundred steps ran straight up to the front of the little shrine—so steep and sudden that we could just look along their edge. From the high rock, recessed, ran back the shore, on which stood in a row three large junks with their sterns to the sea—behind them trees and houses. On the opposite side of the little harbor four of our men, up to their middle or up to their armpits in water, slowly dragged our junk nearer to the shore. All was quiet and gray—the men reflected in the moving water, the boat creaking along slowly. As I went up the beach, following our guide and the boatmen, I thought how like this was to the Homeric haven—the grove looking out to sea and frequented by "fowls maritimal"; the sacred rock; the meadows and the little stream; the long galleys drawn up on the beach. The little houses of the fishing-village were surrounded by gardens, and their walls largely made of plaited bamboo. There was no inn, but we found a house half shop, and were welcomed to some tea and to a room which the family hastened to abandon for us. There were only two rooms besides the entrance, which was a large passage floored with earth, and along one side of it a raised surface, from which began the level of our flooring.

Sliding partitions, hurriedly run up, made us a room, but the outside screens were full of holes, through which, in a few minutes, peered all the women and children of the village, who occasionally even pushed aside the screens to see more completely. The little passage in front of our open room was filled with girls and children intent upon our ways of smoking, of taking tea, and of eating—for we had biscuits with us, and fifteen hours at least without food had made us fairly hungry. Meanwhile the men landed their wagons and the trunks, and took their meal of rice, hastily made up, on the ledge of the platform on which we sat. This they did in a row, the whole twenty eating quietly but rapidly,—I was going to say firmly,—shoving into their mouths the rice from the bowls, and tearing with their fingers the fish just cooked. Meanwhile, among all the ugliness around us in women, shone out, with beautiful complexions,—lost in the others by exposure to wind and sun, by hard work, and probably by child-bearing,—three girls, who stood before us a long time, with sweet faces and bright eyes and teeth. They stared hard at us until stared at in return, when they dispersed, to watch us again like children from the doors and from the kitchen.

Our hostess, small, fat, good-natured, and polite, showing black-lacquered teeth between rosy lips, like ripe seeds in a watermelon, bustled about hurrying everything, and at the end of our meal our host appeared—from the kitchen apparently—and knelt before us. Poor and ragged as the house was, with ceilings black with age and smoke, and screens torn and worn by rubbing, the little *tokonoma* held a fairly good picture, and a pretty vase with flowers below it. But it was evidently one of the poorest of places, and had never seen a foreigner in it. This may have been the cause of the appearance of the ubiquitous Japanese policeman within five minutes of our arrival. He alone betrayed no curiosity, and disappeared with dignity on getting our credentials.

The rain still held off. We entered our kurumas, now ready, and hastened to the main road which we were to find at Numadsu, if that be the name of the place. But, alas! the rain came down, and my views were confined within the outline of an umbrella. My only adventure was stopping at some hovel on the road to buy some more of that heavy yellow oiled paper which replaces the leather apron that we usually find attached to our European carriages. By and by I consented to have the hood of my wagon put up, through which I could see little more than the thatched backs of my runners, their bowls of hats, off which the rain spattered upon their straw cloaks and aprons, and their wet brown legs, lifted with the regularity of automatons. It was getting cold, too, and women under their umbrellas wore the graceful short overcoat they call *haori*, and tottered over the wet ground on high wooden pattens.

This I noticed as we came into Mishima, from which place we were to begin our ascent up the Hakone Pass. On our way, were it to clear, we might see Fuji again—at any rate, if it cleared in the least we would enjoy the mountains. Meanwhile we shivered at lunch, trying to get into corners where the wind would not leak through the cracks of the shojis, and beginning to experience the discomforts of Japanese inns. And now my bashfulness having gradually abandoned me, I could take my hot bath, separated from the household by a screen not over high, over which the fat servant-girls kindly handed me my towels. Excuse these trivial details, but I cannot otherwise give you the "local color," and my journal is one of small things. Had I come here in the old days when I first fell in love with Japan, I might have met with some thrilling experience in an inn.

I might have had such an experience as our poor friend Fauvel met with not far from here. I might have met some young sworded men, anxious to maintain their dignity and ripe for a quarrel with the foreigner. Do you remember that he jostled the sword of some youngster—"the sword, the soul of the Samurai"—which its owner had left upon the floor. The insult would have been impossible to explain away had not some sensible Japanese official decided that a man who was so careless with his sword as to leave it on the mat, instead of on the reputable sword-rack, had no right to complain of another's inadvertence.

I sometimes wonder which of the courteous persons I meet, when age allows the supposition, obeyed these rules when they were younger; which ones now dressed in black broadcloth wore the great helmet with branching horns, or strapped the two great swords at their waist. And I am lost in respect and bewilderment to think that all this wondrous change—as great as any that the world can have seen—was effected with such success and accepted in such a lofty spirit.

We were now to give up the kuruma and to travel by the kago, which, you will remember, I promised to describe. The kago is a curious institution, partly superseded by the kuruma, but lingering in many places, and necessary where the pack-horse would be unsafe, and where one would otherwise have to walk. It consists of a small litter hung by stiff bamboos from a great pole, over which is steadied a little matted roof, from which various protections from rain or sun can be dropped. The kago has its discomforts: one lies down in it all doubled up, with legs crossed as far as they can be made to, because the basket, which is the body of the litter, is only about three feet long; and with head to one side, because, if one lifted it, it might strike the ridge-pole. The proper way is to lie not quite in the axis. This is all the more natural, as the men at either end do not carry it in a straight line, but at an angle, so that from one side you can see a little in front of you.

Into the kagos we were folded, and in a torrent of rain we departed. I resisted my being shut up in my litter by the oiled-paper sides that are used in the rain, and I depended upon mackintosh and blanket to protect me. The rain came down in sheets. We trotted uphill, the men going on for a few minutes, then changing shoulders, and then again another pair taking their turn—four to each litter. Meanwhile they sang, as they trotted, something which sounded like "Hey, hey, hey, het tue hey." The road was almost all paved, and in the steeper ascents was very bad.

And now I began to experience some novel sensations not easy to describe. My feet were turned in upon the calves of the legs like an Indian Buddha's, and I soon began to ache along sciatic lines; then elsewhere, then everywhere. Then I determined to break with this arrangement, as anger seized me; fortunately a sort of paralysis set in, and I became torpid and gradually resigned; and gradually also I fell asleep with the curious motion and the chant of the men, and woke accustomed, and so I am writing.

I can just remember large trees and roads protected by

them; some places where we seemed alone in the world, where we left trees and stood in some narrow path, just able to see above its sides—all else shut out of existence by the rain; and I have all along enjoyed the novel sensation of moving on the level of the plants and shrubs.

We now are going downhill again, and can look down an avenue of great trees and many steps which we descend. We are coming to Hakone; I can see the lake beyond a Torii, and at the first corner of the road under the trees begins the village.

MIYANOSHITA, September 28.

Again the kago, and the rain as soon as we departed. I turned as well as I could, to find the lovely lines, now lost in general shapes and values, blurred into masses. Once the light opened on the top of some high hill, and I could see, with wild roses right against me, some flat milestone marked with an image against the edges of distant mountains, and a sky of faint twilight pink; or again we pattered along in wet grass, past a great rock with a great bas-relief image—a Jizo (patron of travelers) sitting in the loneliness with a few flowers before him. Then in the rain, and mingling with the mist, thicker cloudings marked the steam from hot springs, which make these parts of the mountains a resort for invalids and bathers.

Soon the darkness: then pine knots were lighted and we descended among the trees, in a path like a torrent, the water running along between the stones, which the feet of the bearers seemed to find instinctively. The arms of the torch-bearers were modeled in wild lights and shadows; the hats of the men made a dusky halo around their heads; the rain-coats of straw glistened with wet; occasionally some branch came out, distinct in every leaf, between the smoke and the big sparks and embers. The noise of torrents near by rose above the rain and the patter and the song of the men. The steepness of the path seemed only to increase the rapidity of our runners, who bounded along from stone to stone. After a time anxiety was lost in the excitement of the thing and in our success, but quite late in our course I heard behind me a commotion—one of A——'s runners had slipped and the kago had come down; no one hurt—the kago keeps its occupant packed too tightly. Then the path left the wild descent; we trotted through regular, muddy roads, stopped once on disbanding our torch-bearers, and reached the Europeanized hotel at Miyanoshita, where I intend to sleep to-night on a European bed, with a bureau and a looking-glass in my room. One little touch not quite like ours, as a gentle lady of uncertain age offers me her services for the relief of fatigue by massage, before I descend to drink Bass's ale in the dining-room, alongside of Britons from the neighboring Yokohama, only one day's journey farther.